PAINTED SONGS & STORIES:

THE HYBRID FLOWERINGS OF CONTEMPORARY PARDHAN GOND ART

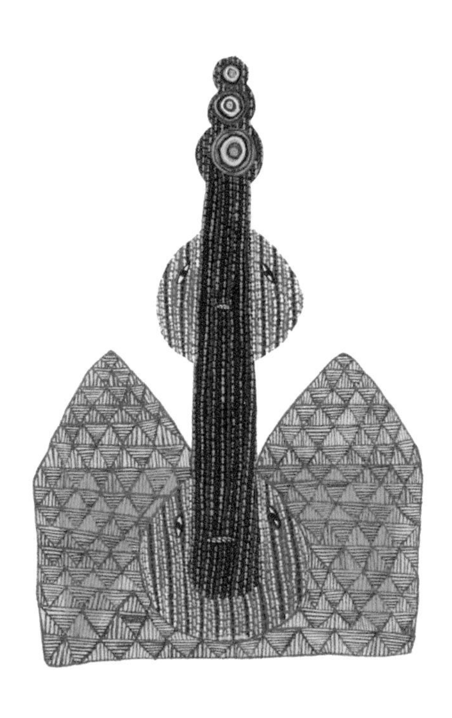

Painted Songs & Stories

The Hybrid Flowerings of Contemporary Pardhan Gond Art

JOHN H. BOWLES

FOREWORD BY PANKAJ MISHRA

With additional contributions by:

Hartosh Singh Bal, Ishwar Dass, Suresh Singh Dhurvey, Shampa Shah, Bhajju Shyam, Jangarh Singh Shyam, Mayank Shyam, Nankusia Shyam, Rajendra Shyam, Venkat Raman Singh Shyam, Rashmi Varma, Dhavat Uikey, Ram Singh Urveti, Durga Bai Vyam and Subhash Vyam

INTACH
BHOPAL CHAPTER

PAINTED SONGS & STORIES:
THE HYBRID FLOWERINGS OF CONTEMPORARY PARDHAN GOND ART

This book has been published in conjunction with the exhibition "Painted Songs and Stories: Contemporary Pardhan Gond Art From India", organized by Wellesley College's South Asia Studies Program, to be shown at The Davis Museum and Cultural Center (April 7 – June 6, 2010), with a satellite display at the Brookline Arts Center (April 11 – May 7, 2010), before travelling on to other venues.

ISBN 978-81-7304-867-8

Published by INTACH (Indian National Trust for Art and Cultural Heritage), Bhopal Chapter
E 1/154 Arera Colony, Bhopal, Madhya Pradesh - 462016, India.

Designed and typeset by Brinda Datta, Seapia Graphics, 2204 Sector D2, Vasant Kunj, New Delhi -110070, India.

Processed, printed and bound by Archana, C-78, Okhla, Phase 1, New Delhi - 110020, India.

Distributed by Manohar Publishers & Distributors, 4753/23 Ansari Road, Daryaganj, New Delhi - 110002, India.

Half-title page: *Shrine of the Mother Goddess* by Ram Singh Urveti, acrylic on paper,1998.

Facing title page: Detail of *The Creation of Bamboo* by Durga Bai Vyam, acrylic on canvas,1998.

Title page: Durga Bai Vyam, Sonpuri, 2006 (mural by Gangaram Vyam; *digna* design in foreground by Durga Bai Vyam).

Opposite page: *Peacock* by Jangarh Singh Shyam, ink on paper,1998.

Page 116: *Chinhari Tree* by Rajendra and Sushila Shyam; ink on paper, 2005

To the memory of

JANGARH SINGH SHYAM
(1960-2001)

and

STUART CARY WELCH
(1928-2008)

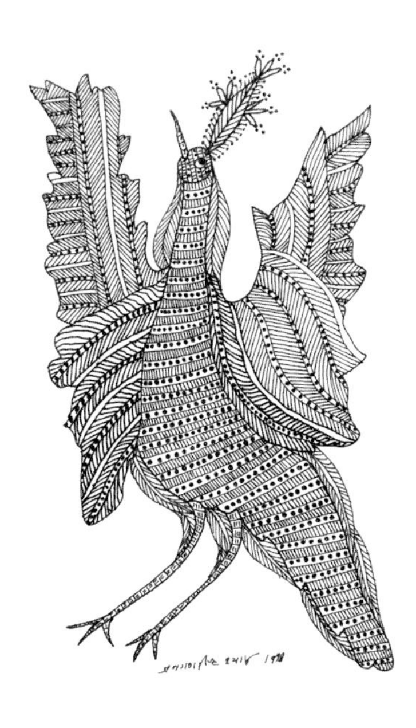

Patharri Chiriya
2000
by Suresh Singh Dhurvey (1977-)
Pen and ink on paper, 11 x 8½"

CONTENTS

ACKNOWLEDGMENTS

Contemporary Gond artists often end up excluded from serious discourse about their work, and can feel unfairly handicapped by their inability to represent themselves and their ideas. According to the Gond artist Venkat Raman Singh Shyam:

> "The difference in how our arts are assessed has more to do with verbal sophistication rather than artistic talent. The non-tribal artist can express himself in a language and an idiom that does not come naturally to a tribal artist—and here [in India] that means English. I may be able to express myself clearly in Hindi, and have a clear idea of what I'm doing, but how many in our art world can follow Hindi? I feel rather ashamed to say this, but this is the truth."[1]

Clearly those of us who speak one or more of the art world's elite languages of power and authority—be it the current jargon of museums and academia, or plain English—must proceed with due care and respect when presuming to represent the work of any contemporary tribal artists. Indeed, the ways in which such arts are represented in public exhibitions contributes towards how whole tribal cultures are generally perceived by the world at large.[2] One must trust that, over the course of time, misrepresentations will be ameliorated, especially as tribals and other subjugated or marginalized communities become increasingly involved in art criticism and curatorial processes—including interpreting, "contextualizing" and generally representing themselves.[3]

The art historian Joseph Alsop has noted a "...Siamese twin-like shared bloodstream of ideas and viewpoints which always flows back and forth between art collecting and art history."[4] Thus my own dual role—as both collector of these artworks and curator of this exhibition—must also be open to examination. Given that public collections and displays of Pardhan Gond art have been relatively inaccessible, limited and/or under-documented, I saw no better way to help preserve, perpetuate and carefully study these arts than to become a patron myself, and in the process attempt to learn as much as possible from the artists while also trying not to interfere with their creative processes. Certainly reciprocal biases, projections and expectations have inevitable influence on the Gond artists' regard for me and other outsiders—and our regard for them and their work. In order to explore our respective self-presentations to (and views of) one another, an academic symposium—"The Gond and Beyond: The Predicament of Contemporary 'Ethnic' Arts"—is being held in conjunction with this collection's exhibition opening. This symposium will offer ample opportunities to explore aesthetic and cultural authenticity, mutual "strategic positioning" and other issues and dynamics involved in the evolution of tribal visual expression created for non-tribal art markets and patronage. It is planned that at least one representative Gond artist will be able to participate at this symposium. Information offered in this publication will doubtless provide further "grist for the mill" at such critical and intellectual occasions.

Yet it bears noting that, however intellectually engaging these artworks may be, this collection was not assembled as an academic exercise. Nor was it acquired as a means of financial speculation (although most of these works were admittedly bought before their artists were widely recognized). Their chief attraction to me as a collector has been a simple and subjective matter of aesthetic delight, and as such it gives great pleasure to share this delight with others. This exhibition also offers an opportunity to muse on these artworks' significance, both in terms of individual iconographies and distinctive styles, as well as in the broader terms of what they may represent—among other things as fine examples of an inventive new hybrid phenomenon, combining tradition-derived content and styles with modern media.

As far as possible, this publication endeavors to present the artists' own accounts of their lives and artworks. To do so—in English (my own Hindi being insufficient for making accurate translations)—we were fortunate to receive invaluable assistance from several individuals of different professional backgrounds and institutional affiliations, in what unexpectedly evolved into a loose-knit collaborative effort. Their respective contributions made this project possible and are duly noted [by bracketed initials] at the end of each catalogue entry. They are: Hartosh Singh Bal [HSB], the Delhi-based writer and journalist, with whom I first journeyed to the Gond villages of eastern Madhya Pradesh, and whose generous knowledge and insights have permeated my own thoughts in ways impossible to credit fully; Dr. Ishwar Dass [ID], convener of the Madhya Pradesh Chapter of the Indian National Trust for Art and Cultural Heritage—who, along with his wife and co-convener Dr. Meera Dass, has provided unstinting hospitality and long-term guidance and patronage to both me and many Gond artists; Shampa Shah [SS], a curator at Bhopal's Indira Gandhi National Museum of Mankind—to whom I owe special thanks for originally introducing me to most of the Gond artists here represented; Dhavat Uikey [DU], a Pardhan Gond and qualified engineer who now devotes much of his time to practicing and promoting Gond art; and Dr. Rashmi Varma [RV], a professor at the University of Warwick and author of her own forthcoming book on contemporary Indian tribal art and culture. My own contributions are also duly identified [JHB], and I bear editorial responsibility for any inadequacies or inaccuracies that may occur in the catalogue entries.

Others in India who have—at various stages of this project—been most helpful and encouraging include Dr. Niranjan Acharya, Sharad Chandra Behar, Arpana Caur, Dr. Kalyan Kumar Charkravarty, Huzoor and Sulakshna Choudhry, Dr. Jyotindra Jain, Mushtaq Khan, Pradip Krishen, Ajit Mishra, Dr. Suresh Mishra, Ritu Mohan, Dr. Alok Rai, Keshav Sharma,

Sachin Vyam, Satish Vyam and Saroj Vyam facilitate the photographing of Durga Bai Vyam's painting of ***Krishna Playing Flute****, Professors Colony, Bhopal, 2009.*

Gulammohammed Sheikh, Manoj Shrivasthava, Harsha Swaminathan, Kalidas Swaminathan, Dr. Kapil Tiwari, Ashok Vajpeyi, Akhilesh and Archana Varma, and Dr. Yoichi Yamagata. Substantial assistance, encouragement and/or support has also come from various individuals outside of India, including Dr. Nancy Berliner, Norma E. Bowles, Norma L. Bowles, Dr. and Mrs. Pramod Chandra, Dr. John Carey, Tara Douglas, Katherine Duffy, Lisa Easley, Dr. Shelly Errington, Dr. Virginia Fields, the Gray Family, Elayne Marquis, Dr. Stephen Markel, Mary Mount, Dr. Geeta Patel, Dr. Carl Pechman, Dr. Julia Shaw, Dr. Neelima Shukla-Bhatt, Jennifer Spoon, Dr. David Szanton, David and Wambui Updike, Edith Welch, Dr. Michael Yorke, Susan Zilber and the late Stuart Cary Welch. Olga Bowles and Edgard Rincon graciously volunteered their professional talents in photographing the artworks and making small but effective "Photoshop" adjustments. Copyediting was expertly done by Nita Sembrowich, and the catalogue's tasteful layout was designed by Brinda Datta. The exhibition's inclusion of animated films (see catalogue Fig. 40) was made possible by the UK-based Adivasi Art Trust and West Highland Animation. I am indeed grateful to Pankaj Mishra for his generous Foreword.

The exhibition that occasions this publication would not have been possible without the enthusiasm and persistent efforts of Dr. Margery Sabin, a co-founder of Wellesley College's newly established South Asia Studies Program—for which "Painted Songs and Stories" serves as its first major visual arts project and symposium. The exhibition was made possible because of much generous support at Wellesley College, including the college's Dean, Dr. Andrew Shennan; the Kathryn Wasserman Davis Fund for World Cultures; the Davis Museum and Cultural Center; and a grant to the college's South Asia Studies Program from the United States Department of Education's Undergraduate International Studies and Foreign Language Program. The Brookline Arts Center's related satellite display of artworks (including Figs. 16 and 18), entitled "The Tribal World of Venkat Raman Singh Shyam", was made possible thanks to the center's director, Susan Navarre, and its board members Manika Srivastav, and Mr. and Mrs. Barnett B. Berliner. The author salutes the Bhopal Chapter of INTACH for all of its generous support over the course of many years, its ready eagerness to publish this catalogue, and its long-term commitment to this and other, similar endeavors through its Tribal Arts and Heritage Projects. Hearty thanks go to my friends Dr. E. Melanie DuPuis, and Jamey and Debi Rosenfield—whose donation was made in honour of Barbara Mann Rosenfield (Wellesley College Class of 1952)—for their respective contributions towards making this publication possible; and fond appreciation to Ruth Nagel Jones (Wellesley College Class of 1942, and my godmother) for all of her memorable support and personal encouragement to me in this and other projects.

Above all, I want to thank my various Pardhan Gond artist friends and their families for all their patient cooperation, generous hospitality, abiding good faith and camaraderie. Foremost among them are the late Jangarh Singh Shyam, his widow Nankusia and son Mayank, Suresh Singh Dhurvey, Bhajju Shyam, Rajendra Shyam, Venkat Raman Singh Shyam, Ram Singh Urveti, Durga Bai Vyam and Subhash Vyam. I trust they will forgive whatever errors have been made here in representing them and their art works. It is hoped that this first American exhibit and catalogue celebrating contemporary Gond art will encourage others to pursue further studies leading towards a greater understanding and appreciation of this unique, traditional yet contemporary and ever-evolving culture.

Anna Dai (Grain Mother)
1998-99
by Suresh Singh Dhurvey
(1977-)
Poster paint on paper
27¼ x 21¼"

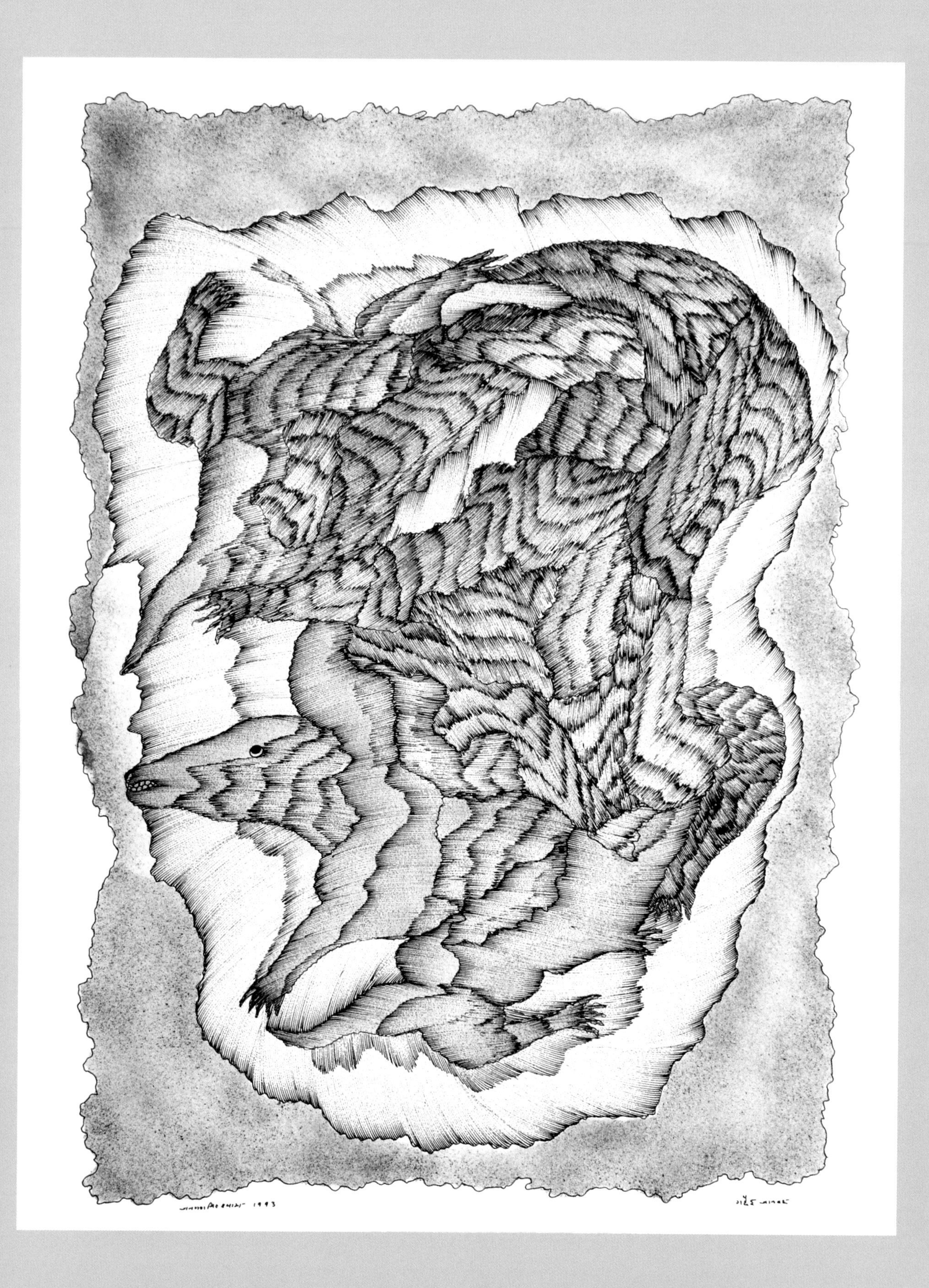

FOREWORD

BY

PANKAJ MISHRA

Travelling in the 1940s to the remotest parts of Asia, Claude Levi-Strauss wondered, with melancholy sigh, how the "proliferating and overexciting civilization of the West" had managed to break "the silence of the seas once and for all." Half a century later, nothing of what the West exported around the world seems to have endured longer than the ideology of "progress": modern man's conceit that humanity is engaged in a continual evolution from "primitive" to a "civilized" existence, and that technology has helped him evolve from "backward" to "advanced" society.

Inconveniently, however, for "evolved" man, his deepening self-regard has coincided with the bloodiest two centuries in history. The unprecedented crimes of "civilized" nations and empires in the modern era confirm that, as Theodor Adorno put it, "no universal history leads from savagery to humanitarianism, but there is one leading from the slingshot to the megaton bomb." Despite his apparently supreme self-confidence, modern man, and his clones in Asia, Africa and Latin America, have often been drawn, by self-doubt and nostalgia, to the figure of the "noble savage".

Rudyard Kipling, arch-imperialist and zealous carrier of the white man's burden, had much more regard for the Gonds, a diverse group of aboriginal people in Central India and the creators of the wonderful art on these pages, than for educated Indians, whom he derided as "babus". In *The Jungle Book* Kipling describes the "tribe of wandering Gonds—little, wise, and very black hunters, living in the deep Jungle, whose fathers came of the oldest race in India—the aboriginal owners of the land."

Monitor Lizards
1993
by Jangarh Singh Shyam
(1960-2001)
Ink and watercolours on paper
24 x 18"

Ironically, it was another product of the British Empire, Verrier Elwin, a former Oxford don and anthropologist, who cut through Kipling's exotic exaggerations, representing the Gonds as a people with their own myths, philosophy, and, indeed, art (a word not used by the Gonds themselves for their everyday visual expressions). In the early part of the 20th century, when Elwin began his investigations in Central India, "primitive" art had acquired a brief vogue; but it was trendy only as long as it featured in the work of a great modernist master like Picasso. On its own, it aroused serious doubts since primitive man was assumed, by general consensus, to languish at the lowest end of the evolutionary scale from his "civilized" counterpart. Elwin vigorously challenged these prejudices, which both Westerners and semi-Westernized Indians shared. Over several books he drew a detailed portrait of the Gonds, openly delighting in their free social and sexual mores, which he vigorously defended from puritanical Hindus as well as Christian missionaries and Victorian-style administrators.

Ashis Nandy has pointed out that if the general rule in the animal kingdom is "eat or be eaten", the one that obtains among humans is "define or be defined". The Gonds may have been lucky to have interlocutors as sympathetic and intellectually nimble as Elwin, and, closer to our time, the Indian painter and curator J. Swaminathan, who materially helped and inspired a new generation of Gond artists in the 1980s. But the ideologies of "progress" have spread more widely since the 1940s and 50s, and the Gonds today can seem to be one of the many laggards in India's apparently relentless march to Western-style development and modernity. Certainly, that's how they seemed to me when I was growing up in Central Indian small towns and even later at university in the 1980s: an impoverished community reduced to working as menial labor or to being at the mercy of markets where they sold what their metropolitan patrons took to be "ethnic arts and crafts". The Gonds seemed doomed. I had no idea that they were in the process of redefining their own art, or that Jangarh Singh Shyam, one of their pioneering modern artists, was even then using commercial paints to depict what had not been depicted before. I had yet to learn that Gonds also possess an old and peculiarly Indian genius for adaptation through hybridization in even the most adverse circumstances. (Not surprisingly, Gond art today is one of the last surviving non-Western arts to be still evolving.)

My own awareness of Gond art, its amazing richness, potential (and pitfalls), came through a fortuitous encounter with John Bowles. When I first met John in the late 1980s, he had just finished producing an exhibition of the contemporary art of yarn paintings as practiced by the Huichol Indians of northwestern Mexico (the Huichols also depict traditional subject matter using modern media). Organized with the ethnographer Juan Negrín, this exhibition toured museums in Europe and then appeared as the first celebration of contemporary tribal artists to be held at Mexico City's Museum of Modern Art. (In the early 1990s John donated his large collection of Huichol art to Radford University Art Museum in Virginia.) He had studied art history at Harvard University with the distinguished Indian scholar Pramod Chandra and the great connoisseur Stuart Cary Welch. Despite these institutional affiliations, John seemed to me a figure from a less professionalized world: a dedicated admirer of traditional ways and expressions that had retained their originality, vitality, and inner spirit against the formidable challenge of a homogenizing modernity.

In India he was drawn to what had preoccupied him in Mexico: recognizing and honouring the lives and works of peoples who, though relegated to the margins, had their own wisdom to contribute to modern urban civilization. Indian contemporary art was then at the early stage of its present vogue in the West; but John was more taken by the relatively obscure folk and tribal arts, and it was early during his long decades in India that he took on the task of learning from and also helping communicate to the wider world the most recent achievements of Gond culture.

John's desire to help Gond artists introduce their work to a wider audience has often seemed to me cussedly contrarian. After all, John himself had learned from his long and often deeply frustrating experience of producing Huichol art exhibitions how the most glorious art by contemporary tribal people could end up being obscured by the fusty conventions of academic art history departments and museums. I recall John telling me about the museum director in Mexico who felt that tribal arts had to be validated by exhibitions abroad before he could propose and accept them for display at his museum.

Of course, such objections immediately appear an instance of babu-style philistinism when you consider the marvelous art on these pages: the peacock who instructs the tribals how to dance as the monsoons arrive; serpents watching over buried treasure; the tiger who combines the features of the sun, moon and many jungle creatures; the bamboo that emerges from the remnants of a cannibalized woman. Humour and lightness alternate with visions of death and calamity, quickening and deepening our sense of wonder; and if the paintings seem to defy convention, it may be worth reflecting on these famously passionately lines by Goethe, defending the "Gothic" when it was associated with barbarism and the savage:

> "And thus the savage may use weird lines, horrible shapes, strident colours for a coconut, feathers or his own body. However arbitrary these forms, they will harmonise without his knowing anything about the laws of proportion, for it was one single emotion that fused them into one significant whole. This significant art is the only true one."

Yes, but Gond art has encountered its own share of present-day prejudice against "primitive" art. The partisans of "progress", as Levi-Strauss feared, now flourish in the East as well as the West. This first-ever exhibition of Gond art in the United States—whose catalogue you hold in your hands—will hopefully expose more people in the West to the splendors of Gond paintings, especially after John donates his own collection to museums. In India itself, Jangarh Singh Shyam's extraordinary body of work has yet to be honoured with a retrospective exhibition a decade after his suicide in Japan. Jangarh's life, whose struggles and achievement John's sensitive introduction describes in detail, points to the particular dangers to which tribal artists expose themselves in the modern world as successful innovators. As John puts it, "The number and magnitude of the cultural transitions this community of talented tribals has made over the past decades—moving from isolated villages to Bhopal and establishing themselves in relation to unfamiliar economies, new social environments, institutions, professions, and lifestyles—can hardly be grasped by those of us born into urban modernity."

It remains to be seen what this painful transition will result in (and I detect a somber ambiguity even in John's introduction): it may bring about either greater commercialization of Gond art through the vagaries of a globalized art market and high-end consumerism, or it may enhance Gond art's capacity to renew itself, as it must, while keeping alive its vital connection with the past. Certainly, as the crisis of a disenchanted modernity deepens, "civilized" man will be drawn again to the wisdom of his "primitive" peers, who have miraculously survived the near-destruction of their environment. Nothing will help him appreciate the Gond and his worldview more than the art in these pages, beautiful and marvelously alive and always with a spirit of its own.

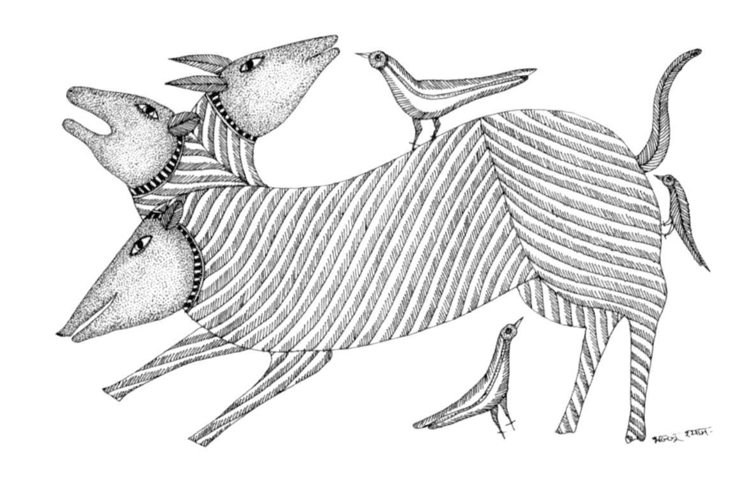

Three Headed Pig
1999
by Bhajju Shyam
(1971-)
Pen and ink on paper
6 x 9.¼"

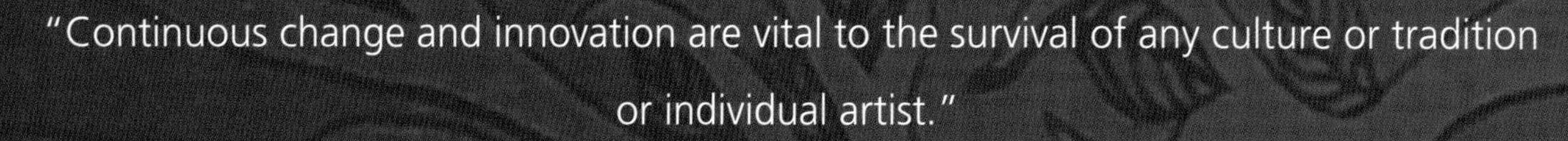

"Continuous change and innovation are vital to the survival of any culture or tradition or individual artist."

— JYOTINDRA JAIN[5]

Jangarh Singh Shyam and his murals at the Pompidou Centre, Paris, 1989

Jangarh and His Successors:

The Origins and Hybrid Flowerings of Contemporary Pardhan Gond Art

BY JOHN H. BOWLES

The suicide of Jangarh Singh Shyam—the founder of a new art tradition practiced by Pardhan Gond tribals of central India—greatly affected his family and community, and also disrupted a larger sphere of academic and professional complacencies. As noted by the art historian Kavita Singh:

> "Jangarh Singh Shyam is believed to have committed suicide on the first day of July 2001 in the Japanese museum where he was a visiting artist. The shock of his death was all the more keenly felt as Jangarh[6] was significant within India both as an artist and an icon. He was a supremely talented individual whose life's trajectory cut across so many boundaries that theorists and critics were left with the task of reappraising the categories and labels, the schools and strata, through which the art world is ordered and organized."[7]

Exactly who was this iconic artist Jangarh Singh Shyam, and how did his life, tragic death and category-defying accomplishments prove such a confounding challenge to the contemporary art world? To what extent can his struggles be considered emblematic of other contemporary tribal artists in his community and elsewhere—and what roles have non-tribal patronage and other such "outside" influences played in these developments? While there can be no complete answers to such questions, by briefly exploring Jangarh's distinctive tribal origins and remarkable career, we can better appreciate his achievements and understand his influence on the other artists from his community here presented—all of whom became artists because of his example, encouragement and assistance. In the course of considering these artists' individual careers and accomplishments, a broad range of issues emerges regarding cultural hybridity and the reinvention of tradition in our times. This brief introductory essay can only touch upon these issues, which will be explored in greater depth at the symposium associated with this exhibition.

An Oral Tradition Evolves into a Narrative Visual Art

Jangarh belonged to a particular Gond *gotra* (clan) called Pardhan. The Pardhans traditionally marry within their clan and serve the larger tribal community as musicians and bardic priests, as well as keepers of genealogies and sacred myths. These oral histories include accounts of the origins of the earth and cosmos, regional flora, fauna and sacred geography, as well as the heroic deeds of great Gond rulers of the past (some historical, others mythological)—all topics central to Gond cosmology and identity. The Pardhan Gonds originally made their living from donations presented in gratitude for their ritual recitations, which were always accompanied by performances on the *bana*, an ancient three-stringed musical instrument venerated as an actual manifestation of the Gonds' supreme deity, Bara Deo. The origin myth about Bara Deo's first manifestation as the *bana* also relates to the creation of the Pardhans and other Gond clans (and is here recounted in the text accompanying Fig. 23. (pages 74 to 75). To this day, much respect and ritual are shown towards the *bana* and its performances, which accompany recitations at ceremonial functions at the homes of regular patrons belonging to other Gond clans—who the Pardhan Gonds traditionally visit during itinerant circuits (called *mangteri*), made every third year. Sometimes these patrons lived several hundred kilometers away, necessitating journeys of many months' duration. Periodic evocations of Bara Deo and other Gond deities were widely considered necessary to avoid adversities; if they were unduly delayed, the Pardhan Gonds would be summoned from afar. In certain ritual performances, their evocations facilitated communication with the divinities through possession of one or more of the assembled listeners.

Ram Prasad Dhruve, master Pradhan Gond bard and performer of the bana. *Such performances involve ritual invocations of Bara Deo, the lighting of incense and* diwa *(a small lamp), and use of* mahua *(a traditional libation made from distilled flower pressings of the* mahua *tree).*

Although these traditions, myths and stories would eventually be depicted in artworks by Jangarh and his successors, at the time of his birth in 1960 his family—like most Pardhan Gonds living in their eastern Madhya Pradesh village of Patangarh—had ceased following their ancestral vocation as itinerant bardic priests. Periods of extreme poverty, drought and famine[8]—combined with a subsequent steady rise in population and various social disruptions dating back to the early 19th century[9]—had considerable impact on the Pardhan patronage, such that the Pardhans themselves were compelled to take up other, more desperate means of subsistence, as described in this mid-20th century Pardhan Gond account:

> "Our difficulties began when the Hindus and Mussalmans [Muslims] came into the Gond villages and took the fruit of the harvest. The Pardhans, who were entirely dependent on the Gonds, were unable to get support and the only thing to do was to steal. Then came the great famine and the Pardhans could not even find anything to steal and had to go to the Relief Works. But they found that Government only gave rice and this was not good enough, so they began to steal goats and chickens from the officials. After this, when the famine was over, they again began their ordinary method of stealing, but Government was ruthless and drove them to ordinary field-work. Our elders also began to feel ashamed and wanted to become respectable. They formed a

panchayat [village council] and declared that any Pardhans engaged in stealing would be fined. It was the fine imposed by our own people, not the police, that really stopped our criminal work."[10]

Colonial attitudes towards the Gonds ranged from romantic paternalism to unabashed racism. The most popular idealization of the Indian "noble savage" appears in Rudyard Kipling's *The Jungle Book* novels—picturesquely set amid the remote Gond-inhabited Seoni Hills of eastern Madhya Pradesh (where Kipling himself never ventured). Of greater relevance to the Gonds themselves was the British categorization of their communities as "backward", "unclean" or belonging to "depressed classes", and their division into "criminal" and "non-criminal" groups. Indeed, the very application of the English term "tribe" is problematic.[11]

"Gounds" illustrated in an 1876 publication by the French explorer Louis Rousselet.[12]

The Gonds are not easily categorized, and defy the usual generalizations and assumptions made about tribal societies. For one thing, they are more heterogeneous and numerous than is considered typical of a tribal people: as the subcontinent's second largest tribal group, their population now exceeds ten and a half million people dispersed over six contiguous states and is differentiated into dozens of sub-tribes, clans and sub-clans following diverse customs, beliefs and languages. While many Gonds speak variants of a south Indian Dravidian language, known as Gondi, most of the Pardhans and other Gonds of modern-day eastern and central Madhya Pradesh speak regional dialects of Hindi. The Gonds' earliest geographical origins are far from clear. Most scholars believe that they originated in south India and, in pre-historic times, migrated to the centre of the subcontinent.[13] Certainly by the early 15th century they had settled into Maharashtra and Madhya Pradesh, where they established feudal kingdoms and became socially and economically stratified. According to the anthropologist Christoph von Fürer-Heimendorf: "In power and material status, the Gond rajas [kings] of that time were equal to many Hindu princes, and the remnants of their forts speak of their former political importance. Yet at the same time other Gond tribes led the life of shifting cultivators far removed from the centres of higher civilization."[14] The medieval Gond kingdoms were not isolated from other populations, and their history includes military and peaceful interactions with their more powerful neighbors. For example, their struggles against the Mughals date back to 1564, when Emperor Akbar's army invaded and defeated the northern Gond kingdom of Graha-Mandla; and even into the 18th century Gonds fought against fragmented Mughal and Maratha forces.[15] Both Muslim and Hindu influences can be seen in what remains of medieval Gond architecture—now mostly in ruins—and are likewise evident in various aspects of the Gond courts themselves: Maithil Brahmins served as priests and poets in the Graha-Mandla court, and one Gond king distinguished himself by writing Sanskrit verse;[16] their rulers adopted the Hindu and Persian titles of kingship (i.e., *raja* and *shah*), intermarried with Rajputs, and often employed Muslim administrative terms to rule their kingdoms.[17]

In contrast with the aforementioned derogatory British colonial characterizations, Pardhan Gonds have been portrayed in a much more positive light by those who have lived among them. For instance, the Indian social worker Shamrao Hivale—who spent over three decades of his life working in the village of Patangarh—described the Pardhan Gond temperament as more "romantic" than Gonds of other *gotras*:

> "...To the Pardhan a song is more important than a sack of grain and this is ultimately true even though the Pardhan insists on getting what he can from the material world. [...] The Pardhan is [...] quick-witted, humorous and a charming companion. He shines and sparkles in the company of his heavy-going slow-spoken Gond brother. If I have to go on tour I always try to take Pardhan rather than Gond porters with me, for to travel with a party of Pardhans is an unending delight. The long miles are soon forgotten in the ceaseless stream of amusing anecdotes, snatches of song and clever sayings."[18]

In addition to doing social work among the Pardhans, Shamrao Hivale also pursued various folklore and anthropological studies with his famous associate, Verrier Elwin, the controversial English philanthropist and scholar of tribal cultures.[19] Much of what is known about traditional Pardhan Gond culture was first recorded by Hivale and Elwin—the latter of whom was the first European to recognize and patronize certain forms of Gond visual expression as "art".

Clay relief depicting Shiva by Dukhala Bai at Sadwachappar, Madhya Pradesh, 2006.

Instances of Non-tribal Influence and Patronage

Starting in 1932, Elwin and Hivale established ashrams, schools, leper colonies and health clinics in various communities in eastern Madhya Pradesh. Elwin also commissioned talented Gonds to decorate some of these facilities with murals and figurative clay reliefs. He expressly invited Dukhala Bai from the village of Sadwachappar to do clay reliefs at Patangarh, where he and Hivale had moved in 1937. Dukhala Bai was well known for her clay reliefs, which were in great demand throughout the region.[20] One of the Patangarh women who emulated her talents was Adhara Bai Shyam—who would in turn later teach her son Jangarh Singh Shyam how to model clay.[21]

Long before Elwin and Hivale had settled in Patangarh, the village had already experienced non-tribal influences from afar—such as those illustrated in a mural depicting the mid-monsoon feast of Atekanhaiyya, a birthday celebration of Krishna, who is worshipped as an incarnation of Lord Vishnu by many Hindus. The myths and cults of Krishna are not indigenous to the region surrounding Patangarh, but rather to (and further south and west of) ancient Mathura, from whence they spread throughout the subcontinent and beyond.[22] Like many tribal peoples, the Gonds often adopted outside customs and beliefs in ways that either harmonized with their own well-established norms and values, or could be aligned to do so. For example, traditional Gond imagery includes representations of Shiva (see relief by Dukhala Bai shown above)—whom they identify with their own supreme deity Bara Deo ("Great God")—and the much beloved Hindu elephant-headed god

Ganesh. In both cases Puranic Hindu traditional myths[23] and iconography have been blended with uniquely Gond concepts and features—such as can be seen in the depictions of Bara Deo and Ganesh Kekra ("Ganesh the Crab") here presented (see Figs. 21 and 23). In his influential book of 1946, *The Tribal Art of Middle India*, Elwin described a particular Patangarh mural as an amusing instance of the Pardhan's erotic twist of Krishna mythology:

Gond mural in black and red on a white ground, depicting an incident from Krishna's life. Patangarh. Height: 30"

> "The aim of [these] pictures (one of which is reproduced [at right]), while entirely characteristic of the twist given by the tribesmen to many classic themes and customs, is not one which would be approved by the orthodox Hindu. Their purpose is frankly aphrodisiac. Youths offer milk and curds to the pictures and pray, 'As the seven hundred milkmaids followed Krishna, so let the girls of this village follow me.' Girls, making similar offerings, pray in their turn, 'As Krishna loved the milkmaids and never left them, so let the youths of this village love me and never leave me.' The Pardhans tell a story, which does not appear in the Sanskrit records, that when Arjun saw his friend Krishna's stupendous success with young women, while his own hopeless passion for Subhadra remained unrewarded, he grew depressed and jealous. He retired to the forest and on the walls of his hut painted the first originals of the pictures made in a thousand homes today, exclaiming, 'O Krishna, you are loved by seven hundred, but not a single one loves me.' Krishna's heart was touched by the prayer and the pictures and he granted his friend's wish and brought him and Subhadra together."[24]

Drawing on the same narrative as the Sanskritic tradition, the Gonds give their account a distinctive interpretation that reflects a strikingly different worldview from their elite Brahmanical counterparts.

Other illustrations in Elwin's book include Gond jewelry and tattoos (later to become the basis for innovative design techniques for contemporary painting), wood carvings, as well as murals and clay reliefs applied to their homes and granaries—all presented (with similar examples from other tribes) as "art", a concept alien to the villagers of Patangarh and never before seriously applied to Gond-produced objects and images. As in most traditional societies in Asia and elsewhere, visual expression was so integrated within various other aspects of daily life and culture that the Gond had no equivalent word for "art"—a foreign term and concept introduced to India by European traders and colonials. Anthropologists working in India had typically avoided applying the term "art" to tribal artifacts and material culture.[25] Elwin's description and illustration of Patangarh's Atekanhaiyya festival is approvingly followed by other murals showing more recent forms of modern assimilation by Orissa's Saora tribals: in the midst of "traditional" scenes appear ingenuous depictions of motor cars, a train, bicycle, guns and airplanes (as would crop up again decades later in the paintings of Jangarh and other contemporary Gond artists)—indicating Elwin's awareness of traditional art's natural capacity to integrate outside influences. Yet Elwin could hardly have foreseen how, over thirty years later, another agent of modern outside patronage and influence would arrive in Patangarh from Bhopal and recognize the talent of a local youth, whose subsequent success as an "artist" would later generate a new and unprecedented Pardhan Gond art movement.

The Discovery, Success and Tragedy of Jangarh

According to his widow Nankusia, Jangarh casually pursued various forms of artistic expression before he was "discovered" in October 1981 by a team of visiting talent scouts from afar:

> "Although at that time there were no coloured paints in the village, he used to do *mitti ka kam* [terracotta reliefs] on the walls, as well as make statues out of clay. He was also very fond of playing the flute and other instruments; I still have those instruments lying about with me. Seeing one of his paintings on the wall —I think it was a picture of Hanuman [the Hindu monkey god] ... they asked the villagers about who had done it. Jangarh was out at work somewhere, so they left a canvas and paints and said that they'd come back in fifteen days and that meanwhile he should paint something. I don't know what he painted, but fifteen days later—when they came back—they told my mother-in-law: 'Give this boy to us.'"[26]

These talent scouts[27] had been sent on an official assignment from Bhopal, the capital of the state of Madhya Pradesh, where a cultural institute named Bharat Bhavan ("India Building") was being established to serve as the state's new centre for literary, visual and performing arts. The population of Madhya Pradesh included the nation's largest tribal population, who represented a significant and growing political presence, and whose artistic accomplishments thus needed to be displayed at the inauguration of the new centre's galleries. Bharat Bhavan's first director—Jagdish Swaminathan, one of modern India's leading "Primitivist" artists—was deeply appreciative of India's folk and tribal heritage, especially the latter for its great spontaneity and relative freedom from hierarchical mainstream social and visual conventions. Yet neither Swaminathan nor anyone else in the city knew the particular identities or whereabouts of the state's most accomplished rural artists. Thus he decided to send out teams of Bharat Bhavan assistants and art students to search the hinterlands for master artists and craftspersons and, if possible, bring them and/or examples of their work back to Bhopal.

J. Swaminathan with Baiga tribals in District Mandla, Madhya Pradesh.

At that time Jangarh was just twenty-one years old, meagerly supporting himself and his family by doing drought relief labour—manually digging and transporting soil for small daily wages proffered by a government employment scheme targeting afflicted rural communities. Jangarh had never imagined that a livelihood could be made from painting pictures; nor had he ever seen colours as bright as the commercial poster paints he had been given by Swaminathan's talent scouts.

Jangarh's first sample paintings in commercial paints on paper were brought back to Bhopal to be shown to Swaminathan, who was so impressed that he included them at Bharat Bhavan's February 1982 inaugural exhibition—and this initial and subsequent recognition of Jangarh's genius then entered local lore as a kind of miraculous intervention. Within three months of the exhibition, Swaminathan arranged for a jeep and driver to take him to Patangarh so that he could personally invite Jangarh back to Bhopal to work as an artist at Bharat Bhavan. Although Jangarh had never before left his remote rural homeland, or visited a big city, he immediately accepted the invitation and hopped into the jeep; when Swaminathan urged him at least to inform his family about his departure, Jangarh insisted that that was not necessary—and that they should just go.[28]

Upon arriving in Bhopal, Swaminathan arranged for Jangarh's employment at Bharat Bhavan's graphic arts department, provided accommodations in his own home in Professors Colony, and then eventually settled Jangarh and his family into a modest place of their own in a back alley directly behind his house. Thereafter—with Swaminathan's help and guidance—Jangarh launched himself into an astonishing career. Within the course of twenty years he had been commissioned to do the exterior murals for Vidhan Bhavan (the state's new parliament building which, like Bharat Bhavan, was designed by the renowned architect Charles Correa), went to Paris in 1989 to participate in the Pompidou Centre's *Magiciens de la Terre* exhibition, and travelled thrice to Japan, where he exhibited as an artist-in-residence—first at Saitama's Museum of Modern Art and twice thereafter at the Mithila Museum, in Tokamachi.[29]

Over the course of two decades, Jangarh evolved various styles in different media, ranging from simple pen and ink drawings on paper and small terracotta figures to more ambitious acrylic paintings on canvas, silkscreen prints, large-scale murals and terracotta sculptures. His earliest works—mostly images of Gond divinities who had never before been depicted—are among some of his most powerful works; those few now in public collections[30] show the excitement and force of his creativity, giving form and colour to what was previously invisible. According to his friend and colleague, the artist and art historian Gulammohammed Sheikh, when the talent scouts visiting Patangarh first exposed him to bright commercial paints, Jangarh recalled "...how awestruck he felt by the brilliance of these pigments—just touching them sent tremors through his hands."[31] He increasingly came to enliven his images with the liberal application of coloured dots, which he used to represent jewelry and clothes, or simply as a kind of glitter and sparkle superimposed on silhouetted (and mostly symmetrical) figural representations. While this dazzling use of dots was also practiced by other tribal artists at Bharat Bhavan (and a small controversy continues to this day as to whom should be credited for first using this technique), no one contests that it was Jangarh who developed it into a new, astonishing range of unprecedented effects.

Jangarh also employed other distinctive patterns devised to "fill in" figurative compositions: e.g., fields of dense crosshatching, tightly drawn comb-lines, rows of tiny ovals, bands of dots, sometimes accompanied by narrow squiggles and small irregular amoeba-like forms. He mostly used these pattern fields—variously presented in diagonal bands, semi-circular "fish-scale" patterns or in more irregular/jagged arrangements—to articulate figural forms. Occasionally he surrounded depicted figures with fine lines radiating out from their peripheral contours—to suggest either movement or a sense of resonating presence (see page 12 and Figs. 3 and 6). He also experimented with bold and jazzy interlocking black-and-white stripes, wonderfully voluptuous swirls and colourful speckling techniques (as shown in the ink drawings on page 12 and 25, and Figs. 2 and 3). The artworks presented here show only some of Jangarh's large repertoire of patterns: techniques of enchantment which he uses to invest—or reveal—a dazzling sense of wonderment. In the words of Sheikh: "The repetition of pattern [...] is meant to change the form to assume volume, to expand, turn, move in directions desired [...] to hint at those aspects of the numinous that reveal its wondrous elements: embodying as if through repeating a chant."[32]

While working at Bharat Bhavan, Jangarh befriended another contemporary urban artist Akhilesh Varma, who Swaminathan had appointed to supervise and counsel the visiting rural artists-in-residence. Deeply admiring of Jangarh's early achievements, Akhilesh observed a gradual but certain decline in the vigour and spirit of both Jangarh's artistic expression and, indeed, his very being; and Jangarh's style and choice of subject matter shifted from powerfully raw renderings of his village deities to more charming depictions of flora and fauna.[33] According to Akhilesh:

> "Jangarh was not able to adjust to living in a city; and that was his downfall as a painter. His paintings increasingly featured repetitious embellishments that conveyed *jadta* [inertness], and became more superficially appealing and—in a word—decorative. He was already a famous painter, and had so many commissions—from private patrons, and museums too—and this workload distracted him from his real artistic expression. He started taking help from his community. Young assistants would come to live with him. At first they would do nothing, and then he'd get them involved painting backgrounds, then the figures, and finally Jangarh ended up doing only the finishing touches. In addition to this workload there were also family pressures. Often his wife would be cooking food for up to twenty people who had come to Bhopal to live with them. They had left their villages and came to their uncle, and were dependent on him. So he had to accept more invitations and commissions to earn the money to look after them. And all this eventually made him very depressed."[34]

It was while doing his second artist-in-residency at Japan's Mithila Museum in July 2001 that Jangarh committed suicide. The circumstances surrounding this tragedy remain murky to this day: accounts proposed by the Mithila Museum officials conflict with those offered by various persons and concerned officials in Delhi,[35] and by Jangarh's own family and relatives. According to Jangarh's widow, Nankusia (who kept in touch with Jangarh in Japan by post and occasional phone calls):

> "He would say that I'm working day and night, but that they've given me such huge canvases that it's becoming difficult to finish the work. After the news [of his suicide] nobody in Japan contacted us. I even called the madam in Calcutta [who promoted and coordinated Jangarh's trip to Japan[36]], but she didn't even pick up her mobile phone. Not even in writing did they ever tell me. This is something that is still troubling my heart. What is it exactly that had happened, and what are the reasons that it had happened? We never did find out."[37]

His family and some supporters have blamed the Mithila Museum for underpaying artists-in-residence and exploiting them by retaining their passports, instructing them to extend their visits, and denying them a share of the profits when their work is sold. In the case of Jangarh, the museum's proposed cremation of his remains in Japan—rather than having them sent back to Bhopal for a funeral attended by his family and community (as eventually came to pass)—became a further source of contention, frustration and suspicion among Jangarh's Indian associates, friends and relatives.[38] On their behalf, many leading Indian artists and intellectuals petitioned the Indian government to pursue a thorough inquest, which was never done. In 2002, the Mithila Museum offered its own contrasting account of how the tragedy transpired, in the form of a website posting authored by Curator Miyoko Hasunuma.[39] Among other things, this account mentioned certain "anti-depression" medicines found among Jangarh's personal effects by the museum staff after he committed suicide.[40] The museum defended itself against criticism of exploitation and pleaded ignorance of any prior or ongoing medical condition. In India, the museum's position is basically supported by Akhilesh and his wife Archana, to whom Jangarh occasionally confided his anxieties over "...the increasing demand for his paintings in the market, and [...] his increasing responsibilities towards his family."[41] Akhilesh had referred Jangarh to a local doctor—who prescribed anti-anxiety medications to him.[42]

As time goes on, it becomes ever more difficult to determine what factors may have most contributed to Jangarh's suicide. Unquestionably, medical and deeply personal issues were involved which go beyond the responsibility or culpability of any hosting institution. That certain museums have at times treated tribal artists rather shabbily is undeniable[43]—but this seems unlikely to have happened at the Mithila Museum, given its past and continuing record hosting other visiting artists from rural India. Still, the Mithila Museum's sale of works produced by resident contemporary artists also exhibited in their galleries inevitably renders the museum vulnerable to allegations of exploitation. Policies regarding such practices vary broadly between different museums and nations, and it has been suggested that more formal arrangements need to be developed and implemented for safeguarding the welfare and interests of tribal and folk artists at hosting institutions.[44] While the international presentation of contemporary tribal art and artists provide exciting opportunities to both viewers and artists, the ethical, economic and psychological implications of such occasions have also increased in the aftermath of this tragedy.

Crocodiles
2000
by Jangarh Singh Shyam (1960-2001)
Pen and ink on paper
9 x 7"

Jangarh's Successors

Fortunately, Jangarh left behind an enduring legacy, comprised not only of his own artworks in various media, but also of his personal fostering of the art careers of other Gonds. Jangarh encouraged those with talent to leave their impoverished circumstances in the village and move to Bhopal, where he helped them find odd jobs for regular income while giving them additional art-related work to do in his house. All of the Gond artists represented in this publication (and many not included here) give similar accounts of how, after first serving as Jangarh's assistants and apprentices, they were urged by him to go beyond copying his distinctive style to develop their own styles, so that they could establish themselves as independent artists, able to sustain themselves in relative economic security. Some have already gone on to achieve their own remarkable measure of national and international recognition.

It is important to note that most of the artists mentioned in this essay are somehow related to Jangarh (either by marriage or blood).[45] Thus a single extended family can itself be seen as the basis for a particular painting style, as has likewise occurred in Indian courtly and folk art traditions elsewhere.[46] Yet other "non-Pardhan" Gonds have also come to Bhopal to practice these arts too.[47] While this exhibition cannot fully represent the output of the almost fifty Gond artists now living in Bhopal[48]—much less India's overall Gond population of over ten and a half million persons—various levels of state patronage have advanced the pan-Gond identity of these arts,[49] which positions them to play a more prominent role within a larger, burgeoning Gond identity movement with its own social and political ramifications.[50]

Jangarh's successors within the Pardhan Gond art movement emerge, as did Jangarh himself, from the difficult economic and social circumstances afflicting all of India's tribal communities both during and after the colonial era. Reduced to the penury of reliance on casual wage labour in field and roadwork, and sometimes displaced from their traditional dwelling places by official forest management policies, tribals often have only intermittent and truncated opportunities for schooling, leaving little prospect for future betterment either within or outside their communities. Still, their traditional collective identity has been largely sustained through cultural practices of storytelling, domestic rituals, community festivals and domestic arts and crafts. Over the past few decades, state patronage of the Pardhan Gonds' (and other Indian tribal communities') visual and performing arts indicates a broad-spread and growing recognition of tribal people's legitimate place in the complex fabric of Indian culture. Simultaneously, modern developments and state policies increasingly challenge their more traditionally organic lifestyles. Bhopal has played a central role as the centre of training, exhibition and employment in the life stories of all the recognized leading contemporary Pardhan Gond artists. Starting with Jangarh in the early 1980s, the city's Museum of Mankind, Bharat Bhavan, Adhivasi Lok Kala Parishad (Tribal People's Art Council), Tribal Research Institute, Tribal Heritage Museum and other such institutions exemplify the crucial contribution of public patronage to the flowering of contemporary tribal art. At the same time, they also reflect the displacement of this art from its already fragmented and impoverished communities of origin.

A capacity to evolve and adapt to changing circumstances, by accommodating and assimilating sometimes very different and foreign influences, is key to the survival of any traditional culture. This process—variously described as "cross-fertilization", "hybridization", "acculturation" and other terms (some positive, others pejorative, depending on each writer's biases)—is one in which Indian civilization and cultures have proved themselves remarkably adept. The historian D.P. Singhal has observed how "...many unique developments [...] have resulted from the new cross-fertilisation of cultures, reaching out towards the future [...] Apart from its own vitality, the continuity of Indian civilization is largely due to its ability to adapt to alien ideas, harmonise contradictions and mould new thought patterns".[51]

The following biographical accounts of artists represented in this exhibition demonstrate in detail a variety of responses which the Pardhan Gonds share with analogous tribal communities elsewhere in India—and elsewhere in the world (from the aboriginals of Australia to indigenous peoples throughout North and South America)—among whom remarkable opportunities for artistic creativity flourish amidst the relentless onrush of modernization. Although presentations of such artists usually focus on the problems of categorizing their artworks (as "primitive", "tribal", "folk" or "hybrid", etc.), such matters have been carefully explored elsewhere.[52] More rarely discussed are the artists' personal careers and artwork from their own perspectives. Granted, the interview/translation/editing process inevitably colours these verbal self-portraits, yet some of the original sparkle and flash of Pardhan Gond storytelling still comes through.

Ram Singh Urveti at his home in Professors Colony, Bhopal, 1998.

Ram Singh Urveti

After Jangarh, the senior-most Gond artist here represented is Ram Singh Urveti, who was born in Patangarh about 1965[53] as the seventh of eight children. His mother, Balsa Bai, died when he was two years old, and his father, Raghubar Singh, could not afford to send his children to school. So, at the age of twelve, Ram started to work in the fields during the day, and in the evening learned the alphabet and basic reading, writing and arithmetic from a villager. In the early mornings he would regularly gather firewood with his maternal uncle Jangarh, and when it was time to celebrate Ramlila (the village's eight-day festive re-enactment of the Ramayana epic), Jangarh would take the role of Rama and Ram played the role of Sita. Throughout his childhood and youth he enjoyed listening to his grandparents and other Pardhan Gond elders tell stories and sing songs. Such experiences would later inspire his various artworks. Eventually his sisters and their husbands helped him continue his education at various schools in Gorakhpur[54] and Jabalpur, where he studied until he was about nineteen years old—when again financial constraints were such that he had to abandon his education and return to field labour. When he was about twenty or twenty-one years old, he entered into an arranged marriage with Satroopa, a niece of Jangarh's. Ram farmed a field that belonged to Jangarh. As only intermittent, casual employment was available in Patangarh, in 1991 a relative encouraged Jangarh to take Ram to Bhopal, where he might better secure a regular job. During his first weeks in Bhopal, Ram worked for the Forestry Department, building fences and planting trees in the city's Mata Mandir neighborhood. Then he landed another outdoor job, which lasted for three months, at Bhopal's Indira Gandhi National Museum of Mankind, where he cut grass, dug pits and transported loads of bricks in a handcart. Meanwhile, he learned the art of silk screening from Jangarh, and when a job opening came up in the Museum of Mankind's art department he managed to secure employment there (producing posters, greeting cards, invitations and other such materials, as well as working as an office peon, serving tea, delivering papers, etc.). Ram lived at Jangarh's home for about a year, making occasional visits back to Patangarh, until his wife Satroop gave birth to their daughter Ranjita. After four months he moved his small family to Bhopal, and together they settled into other lodgings, nearby but separate from Jangarh's.

Jangarh asked Ram to assist him with his artwork—filling in figures with colours or ink. Ram also did his own paintings, which Jangarh initially sold for as much as Rs 100, thus encouraging Ram to take a greater interest in art as a livelihood. "When I started doing paintings more seriously, Jangarh advised that since I was more keen on painting Gond stories and myths, I should select a motif which is as old as these stories, and that the motif would also serve to identify my paintings. I thought hard for days and felt that my forefathers lived by hunting using bow and arrows and so the arrow head would be an appropriate motif."[55] Ram also alternated this motif with others, including ones he dubbed *mala* (a beaded necklace motif, comprised of tiny aligned circles alternating with rows of straight lines) and *chowk* (small squares comprised of crosshatched lines). In 1993 he completed his first major painting, a depiction of *Narayan Dev* (the god Narayan), and thereafter he painted *Dharti ki Utpatti* (The Creation of the Earth). In 1998, he and Jangarh both submitted paintings to the Lalit Kala Akademi (National Academy of Fine Arts) 41st National Art Exhibition in Delhi. Ram was awarded lifetime membership in the Lalit Kala Akademi for his painting *Shesh Nag Dharti Mata* (Shesh Serpent—Mother of the Earth). According to Ram: "Jangarh felt very happy about it, and said that he'd have a crate of beer for me—to celebrate my getting the award. He patted me on the back and said: 'What I wanted but couldn't get for many years, you were able to get in one! If you go on like this you'll continue rising in life.'"[56]

Ram almost always depicts subjects taken from traditional Gond stories, but when he went to an international artists workshop—hosted in Chennai by an organization named Dakshin Chitra (Southern Picture)—he and the other participants were asked to invent a new story; so he came up with "The Squirrel's Dream" (see right page). The fable-like story tells of a squirrel who feels harassed by life and dreams of becoming a series of other creatures who are in turn harassed by natural predators. Other paintings by Ram draw more closely on traditional Gond narratives. He enjoys depicting the Gond Rajas of the past, and nature and village scenes—including trees, birds, wild and domestic animals, as well as rituals and ceremonies pertaining to birth, marriage and death. Snakes are sacred to the Urveti family's *gotra*[57], so Ram is especially fond of depicting them.

Ram Singh and Gond artists assisted Jangarh with painting two significant mural projects in Bhopal: the first in 1993 at the Indira Gandhi National Museum of Mankind,[58] the second in 1995 at Bhopal's Vidhan Bhavan (the state's main legislature building). The year after Jangarh's death, Ram and Bhajju Shyam were invited to paint murals at the Masala Zone Restaurant, located in the fashionable district of Islington in London.[59] In 2003, Ram and Bhajju Shyam, along with the artist Durga Bai, contributed illustrations to the award-winning children's book *The Night Life of Trees*.[60] Ram Singh Urveti owes the start of his international as well as Indian artistic career to Jangarh; a selection of his artwork was exhibited along with Jangarh's in the 1998 Musée des Arts Decoratifs exhibition entitled "Expeditions Indiennes". Yet over recent years he has developed a variety of new artistic opportunities, and—together with younger Gond artists—has become widely recognized through exhibitions and commissions in India and abroad. At the same time, he continues to earn his livelihood as a daily wage laborer at the Museum of Mankind, and does his artwork "after hours".

(right page)
The Squirrel's Dream
2003
by Ram Singh Urveti
(1965-)
Acrylic on canvas
41¾ x 29 ½"

Suresh Singh Dhurvey

Suresh Singh Dhurvey was born in Patangarh in 1973, the fifth child of impoverished parents. His father did carpentry work, and both parents worked as sharecroppers in other villagers' fields. After completing one more year of primary school, he discontinued his education because his father couldn't afford to purchase the necessary school supplies and uniforms. From the age of six or seven Suresh worked in the fields with his parents—harvesting, winnowing and threshing wheat as a sharecropper—for which he daily earned one and a quarter *paeli* of grain (a *paeli*, or *kuriya*, is an approximately ten-inch-wide wooden bowl). In the summer season he would help build *bandhs* (small agricultural dams for rice paddy irrigation) for Rs 15 daily wages. In his spare time he would go a few kilometers away—into the Dungari jungle—to fetch fuel wood and gather *mehlain* ("elephant creeper" [61]) leaves used by the Dhurvey clan for constructing ropes, plates, cups and umbrellas. Suresh's mother died when he was eleven or twelve years old. When he was about seventeen or eighteen, Suresh moved to Bhopal, where he lived with Jangarh and his family. Initially Suresh assisted Jangarh, filling in his sketches with his signature semi-circular fields of coloured dots (called *bundi ka kam*—"small dot work"). Eventually, Jangarh also encouraged Suresh to do his own artwork after hours, and registered him as an artist at Bhopal's Museum of Mankind, Bharat Bhavan, and the Adivasi Lok Kala Parishad (Tribal People's Art Council). Encouraged by Jangarh, Suresh invented two distinctive patterns for filling in figures (by which his work can now often be readily identified): the *seedhi* and *tirkha* patterns. The Hindi word *seedhi* can be translated as either ladder or stairs, but in this context Suresh specifically refers to a traditional bamboo ladder. It is comprised of narrow bands of colour filled in with aligned pairs of short parallel brush strokes—a pattern he associates with both "...the rungs of a ladder, as recalled in my father's carpentry workshop, and the network of fine lines that radiate from the pores on the skin."[62] *Tirkha* is the Gondi variant for the Hindi word *teer*, meaning "arrow". It consists of narrow bands of diagonal crosshatching alternating with narrow bands of plain colour (see p. 11). In his ink drawings, Suresh also uses his own distinctive *bundi* (small dot) pattern—which he has dubbed *goli* ("bullet")—comprised of small dots enclosed in circles (as shown in Fig. 34).

Suresh Singh Dhurvey, at Bharat Bhavan, Bhopal, 2007.

In 1993 Suresh returned to Patangarh so as to attend to his dying father and to get married. Thereafter he brought his wife Sindia to Bhopal, and since then she has helped him with his art work by filling in figurative areas with his various patterns. Recently he has invented a couple of new techniques, which he alone applies. One includes tinting the paper with different colours of powdered chalk;[63] the other he calls *ghisni* ("rubbing")—which involves carefully smearing wet ink, a technique he discovered by accident and now regularly employs in drawings on paper. He uses *ghisni* to experiment with non-Gondi styles—as in his more "classical" rendition of Ganesh (shown above). The remarkable range of Suresh's various styles can easily be appreciated by comparing this more canonically proportioned figure to his depiction of Thakur Dev, in which he has used both *seedhi* and

(left) A depiction of Ganesh rendered in the artist's "classical" ghisni *style.*
(right) An adivasi *style acrylic on paper depiction of Thakur Dev (a protective Gond village deity).*[64]

tirkha patterns, in accord with his *adivasi* (tribal) style.[65] Suresh comments that, although he personally enjoys working in the "classical" style, from experience he has learned that customers prefer his "tribal" style: "I don't do many paintings in the classical style because they don't sell. The clients say that they can get better paintings in that style from outside [non-tribal artists]. Then I tell them that they should buy elsewhere, and I don't feel bad about it. I strongly believe that an artist should paint according to his own thinking, rather than according to what the client wants. It is for the client to purchase a painting if he likes it. But I do take into account the positive feedback that I get from the clients." Suresh has also explained the proprietary relation each artist has with his distinctive style: "...the Gond painters in Bhopal have each developed their own characteristic style of painting, which cannot be adopted by others—since it would lead to criticism of copying. So among them there's an unspoken understanding that each one should only pursue his or her own style, and not work in another person's style. Sometimes there can be a bit of friction between artists, if one artist's style seems a bit too close to another's. But usually this isn't a big issue."[66]

In 2001, just before Jangarh left on his last trip to Japan, he arranged for Suresh's daily wage employment as a gallery guard at Bhopal's Museum of Mankind—which meant working eight hours a day, five days a week, for Rs 2,000 a month. In 2006 that employment was terminated, a change that Suresh recounts more as liberation than loss: "...I felt that I had been freed from bondage, and that I could take my paintings and do things on my own [...] so now I have all the time [I need] to pursue my artwork—about which I feel very hopeful for the future."

Durga Bai Vyam

Durga Bai Vyam is one of the foremost contemporary Gond women artists. Born in the village of Barbaspur in 1977, by the late 1980s Durga Bai was using natural pigments[67] to create murals and *dignas* (traditional auspicious designs applied to domestic wall and floor surfaces). Her decorations were so admired that she was often asked by others in the village to do them for marriages and other special occasions—such as Janam Ashtami, the celebration of Krishna's birth.[68] Durga Bai's family could not afford to educate her; at an early age she was put to work herding cattle and labouring in other people's fields. At times the family was too poor to afford wheat to make their *chapatis* (thin pads of unleavened bread), but had to subsist on cooked *chichvi* (grains of wild grasses). Durga Bai's own marriage took place when she was about fourteen or fifteen years old. Thereafter she and her husband worked for Rs 10 daily wages offered by local government relief projects. Together they would dig and transport mud for the construction of a dam at Gorakhpur. When they travelled to Bhopal to seek medical attention for one of their children who required surgery, Jangarh (the brother-in-law of Durga Bai's husband) encouraged them to settle into a small compound next door to his home.

Durga Bai's husband, Subhash, started to do artwork while receiving some basic employment at Madhya Pradesh's public relations department. While left on her own at home with the children, Durga Bai herself (who never likes being idle) started to do some painting, which Jangarh noticed and praised. He encouraged her to do more, and to focus on representing traditional Gond subjects. Throughout her childhood, Durga Bai had listened attentively as her grandmother Noni Pareste told all manner of stories. These included various origin myths accounting for the birth of bamboo, the creation of rice, *kodon* (millet) and other grains, and the origins of the Narmada River and other aspects of the local sacred geography. Durga Bai began to draw upon this rich repertory, while also developing her own distinctive style of interwoven coloured patterns, based on a favorite traditional jewelry design. She calls the small pattern she customarily uses to "fill in" her figures *nag mori*, named, she says "...after the auspicious silver armlet in the form of a serpent. The idea for this pattern occurred to me when I thought of my grandmother Noni Paraste, who wore many *nag mori*."[69] During the past six years, Durga has won several awards for her paintings, including Madhya Pradesh's State Award for Outstanding Artist of 2004, and a 2006 scholarship from the Indira Gandhi National Centre for the Arts. She has also contributed illustrations to various publications in English and Hindi,[70] and has travelled abroad to exhibit her paintings at the 2006 Frankfurt Book Fair (as shown at top right).

Durga Bai and Subash Vyam with their family at their home in Bhopal's Professors Colony, 1999. Subhash's sculptures appear in the foreground.

Flying to the Frankfurt Book Fair
2006
by Durga Bai (1977-)
Acrylic on paper
14 x 11"

Subhash Vyam

Durga Bai's husband, Subhash Vyam, does his own drawings and paintings, which have likewise been prominently exhibited abroad. His large untitled painting of an airplane stuck in a tree was included in the 2004-2006 "Edge of Desire: Recent Art in India" exhibition, which toured museums in the United States, Australia, Mexico and India.[71] Durga and Subhash and other family members often assist one another by filling in details of each other's artwork; and in 2009 he and Durga Bai were jointly commissioned by Narayana Press (New Delhi) to illustrate a book on the life of Dr. Bhimrao Ramji Ambedkar, the Dalit political leader during India's freedom struggle, and chief architect of the Indian constitution. Subhash is also well known for his wood sculptures, three of which are included here (at right and Figs. 4 and 25). He is one of the few Bhopal-based Pardhan Gond artists who is equally talented in sculpture, drawing and painting.

Birth of the Sun and the Moon[72]
1999
by Subhash Bai (1970-)
Wood sculpture
19.75 x 5.5 x 4"

Rajendra Shyam

Rajendra Shyam—more familiarly known as "Raju"—was born in Patangarh in 1974, the youngest child in his family.[73] His father earned daily wages from various kinds of manual work, such as erecting telephone poles and tailoring. As a youngster Raju went to school and helped attend the cattle at the end of each day, until he passed the tenth standard. It was then that the tragic death of his older brother struck by lightning brought heavy financial as well as emotional blows to the whole family. As a result, Raju was compelled to work full time as a daily wage labourer doing road construction. When Raju was in his mid-teens his uncle Jangarh encouraged Raju's parents to move to Bhopal; Raju continued living at the village, where—in addition to his daily wage labour—he did both field and house work.

He first met his future wife Sushila when they were students at school, but their desire to wed was complicated by his lack of money and certain clan restrictions forbidding their marriage.[74] When she was fourteen or fifteen years old they eloped and, despite initial objections and controversy, their marriage was eventually accepted and formalized. Raju continued working in other people's fields as well as for daily wages. Eventually he got a job timbering *saal* wood,[75] spent weeks on end away from home working with a team of fellow labourers, and recalls how each night in the jungle was spent exchanging stories around a campfire. His daughter Aarti was born when he was about twenty years old, and he recalls feeling overwhelmed and embarrassed at becoming a father while he was still so young himself.

Sushila and Rajendra Shyam at their home in Bhopal, 2009.

Hearing of employment opportunities in Bhopal, in 1996 he went to his uncle Jangarh's home there and started to look for work. Raju had great difficulties in finding a job, so Jangarh asked him to work as his assistant. Since childhood Raju has been fond of painting *dignas* (auspicious designs) in the village—where his unusual artistic talent was highly praised and in great demand; according to Raju: "...people around in the village would ask why I wasn't born a girl, because I could do it so well; on a daily basis and at every ceremony I would do the decorations and the *dignas*."[76] Although Jangarh and his young male relatives were beginning to pursue art as a vocation in Bhopal, in the village decorative painting is still identified with the female domestic role. Yet Raju reports the village talk as praise, not mockery. After three years living in Jangarh's home and working as his assistant, Raju learned from Ram Singh Urveti about a job opportunity at Bhopal's Museum of Mankind to work as a *chaparasi* (an office attendant whose errands include delivering documents and tea). By the time I met Raju in 2004, his wife and daughter had moved to Bhopal and he was still working as a *chaparasi* at the Museum; but then, like Suresh Singh Dhurvey, he too lost his job at the museum in 2006, and now feels at greater liberty to devote all his time and efforts solely to his art work, and has participated in many exhibitions and workshops.[77]

Raju describes the distinctive pattern style he most often uses for filling in figures as *bandha*—meaning "tied" or "bound"—which evokes the texture of a rope (as shown on the peacock's body and elsewhere in Fig. 22); he has also on occasion used repeated traditional tattoo designs (e.g. within the blue area on p.106). While Rajendra is to date the least recognized of the Gond artists here presented, his inventive creativity warrants greater appreciation. His wife Sushila assists him by anonymously filling in with ink the detailed leafy filigree that often recurs in his works.[78]

Bhajju Shyam

By contrast, the career of Bhajju Shyam—another impoverished nephew of Jangarh's—has been catapulted into astonishing prominence by a series of serendipitous opportunities. Born in 1971 to another family of poor Patangarh farmers, Bhajju Shyam grew up together with two brothers, helping to farm, tend cattle and regularly gather fuel wood from the jungle, which was then many kilometers from the village.[79] His sister helped her mother with chores at home while he and his brothers went to school at Gorakhpur, where he passed the tenth standard. Thereafter his parents could no longer afford to send their sons to school, so Bhajju began working as a daily labourer in the village or at Amarkantak—digging wells and ponds, doing field and road work and planting trees. After his sister married, he and his brothers had to help with cooking and other household chores usually done by womenfolk—including painting the walls of their house with clay colours. According to Bhajju:

> "My mother used to say that there is no other female in the house, and all the other houses have been cleaned and painted, so you boys should assist me. And we used to assist her in painting the walls, and the floor used to be painted by her—because my mother could not reach the walls with her hands. While doing so we would sometimes make a bird or animal. This we used to do on the courtyard walls, as well as on the outside walls. Among the animals we'd paint a tiger, or an antelope, a tree or bird—or a human being, even a dwarf. [...] We used to decorate the *kothis* [granaries] with such paintings too. Sometimes we used to model clay figures as well. We learned by watching our mother and other villagers do these. Whenever a new house was constructed, a mud wall had to be raised, and the outer surface [...] smoothed, for which clay had to be used while the wall was wet, so that it would adhere. [...] And we did the same thing around the door jambs and windows. Then we used to work as labourers on large houses, and make [...] round designs and *dignas*, like my mother used to do; [and] we tried to do something other than what my mother or the other villagers would do [...] The figures were modeled on the mud walls and [...] then we put colours on those figures; [...] that was my first [art] work. At that time I must have been ten or eleven years old."[80]

In his late teens Bhajju moved to the city of Jabalpur, where he worked for two years doing various jobs (such as mixing and carrying mortar at construction sites, filling up potholes on road repair projects and as a *chowkidar* [watchman]).

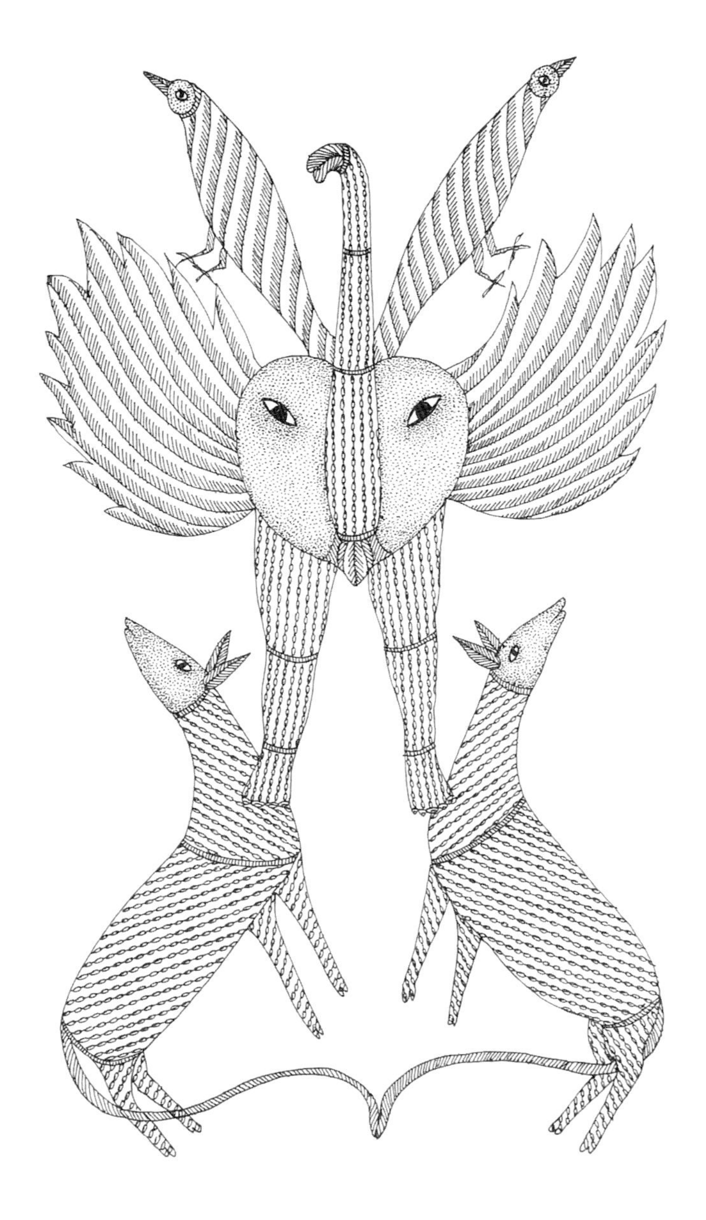

Pen and ink drawing (2002), and detail—showing alternating small oval-and-dash motif, by Bhajju Shyam. Such motifs bear striking resemblance to traditional Gond tattoos.

By 1990, he too had moved to Bhopal where he initially worked as a night watchman for the Indian Institute of Forest Management. But it was lonely and disagreeable work, in which Bhajju regularly encountered porcupines and swarms of mosquitoes. After two months he abandoned it altogether. Bhajju then moved into his uncle Jangarh's home, where he helped with the cooking and other household chores. Gradually he joined other of Jangarh's assistants, filling in sketches with painted designs. Eventually Jangarh encouraged Bhajju also to paint in his own style, and helped him sell his work in Bhopal and Delhi. By the age of nineteen Bhajju was married. He and his wife Deepa took up residence in a nearby garage belonging to a government officer for whom Deepa did housekeeping, while Bhajju worked during the day as a cloth salesman while continuing to paint after hours. Over the course of the following decade Bhajju focused increasingly on art, both in terms of his own painting and as an assistant to Jangarh on particular projects, such as the aforementioned Vidhan Bhavan murals.

The distinctive pattern field Bhajju invented for filling in figures (in his own artworks) is comprised of parallel rows of alternating small ovals and dashes, which he explains is like the Saila dance, in which dancers interlock with one another—the oval-and-dash pattern indicating alternating heads and arms. Bhajju received helpful patronage from both foreign and Indian connoisseurs, notably the Frenchman Hervé Perdriolle, then proprietor of the Outsider Art Gallery in Pondicherry, and the Delhi-based designer and cultural impresario Rajeev Sethi, who Bhajju met through Jangarh. Sethi had been approached by a London restaurateur for recommendations of talented tribal artists to do murals at his Masala Zone restaurant in the city's fashionable Islington suburb. Bhajju Shyam and Ram Singh Urveti were selected and offered a joint commission. This all transpired in 2002, the year after Jangarh's tragic death in Japan; despite broad community misgivings about the dangers of travel and work abroad, Bhajju and Ram accepted the commission, thus initiating a new phase of Gond art expression and international patronage.

The earliest recorded instance of Indian tribals visiting London was at the 1851 "Great Exhibition" held in South Kensington's Crystal Palace—where various "specimens" of primitive cultures were imported from British colonies and put on display.[81] By contrast, Bhajju and Ram arrived in the erstwhile imperial capital as well-recommended, commissioned artists—and private Indian citizens—making their first trip abroad. After completing the restaurant's murals, they spent a few days touring around the city before returning to India. Their experiences abroad later made them into minor celebrities back home, where their families and communities plied them with questions about their impressions of London. Although Bhajju's abilities as a witty raconteur flourished among local spellbound audiences, little did he imagine just how widely known his adventures would soon become through his captivating and humorous visual depictions.

About a year after he returned from London, Bhajju and a couple of Gond artists were invited to Chennai to attend an artists' workshop organized by Tara Publications. Headed by the author and publishing entrepreneur Sirish Rao, the London-based Tara Publications was then in the process of establishing its award-winning reputation for producing elegant children's books, many of which have been illustrated by various contemporary Indian tribal and folk artists. Having heard that Bhajju had recently been abroad, Rao asked him to tell of his adventures in London and then proposed that they collaborate in producing an illustrated account of Bhajju's trip. This resulted in the 2004 publication of *The London Jungle Book*[82]—an illustrated travelogue which returns Kipling's colonial gaze from a humorous, post-colonial perspective. Its illustrations include Bhajju's flight to London in a jumbo jet, shown as a flying elephant (a figure also found in various ancient Hindu and tribal mythologies[83]); London's underground transit system, depicted as a subterranean network of snake tunnels; a multi-armed "Goddess of London", representing the multi-tasking abilities of English women at work; and Bhajju's encounter with an exhibit installation by the contemporary British artist Damien Hirst (in which a bisected cow, displayed in formaldehyde-filled glass cases, is represented according to basic traditional Gond beliefs about reincarnation and the natural cycles of life and death). The good humour, wit and decorative élan of Bhajju's illustrations combine naïve wonder with a sophisticated poise in the face of the Western metropolis. Their appeal to adults as well as children suggests the potential of traditional Gond techniques and designs for expressing original responses to urban modernity. Endorsed by such European intellectuals as John Berger and Roberto Calasso, the book's success led to its translation into four languages, along with further illustration commissions for Bhajju and other Gond artists.[84] Such developments brought renewed hope to the larger community of Gond artists, who had been so demoralized by Jangarh's still recent suicide: once again it seemed that significant recognition and success could be grasped by those willing to innovate or collaborate with "outsiders".

Bhajju Shyam's depiction of a jackal couple, which would later be adapted to serve as the "Drunken Fox" pub sign featured in one of the artist's The London Jungle Book *illustrations. Acrylic on paper, 7 ½ x 10 ¼", 2004.*

In addition to continuing his imaginative collaborations with Sirish Rao, Bhajju also continues to paint depictions of traditional Gond stories and subject matter (such as Figs. 9 and 10). His artwork has been exhibited at galleries, museums and other prestigious venues in India and Europe.[85]

Venkat Raman Singh Shyam

The final Gond painter to be presented here is another nephew of Jangarh's, Venkat Raman Singh Shyam. Venkat has a remarkable memory regarding both traditional Gond stories in general, and the details of his own life's various struggles and career experiences in particular.[86] Born in 1970 in the village of Sijhora (located about 80 km southeast of Patangarh), Venkat attended school until he reached the sixth standard, at which point he dropped his studies so as to accompany his father—Pyare Lal Shyam—to Dindori, where Pyare Lal had gone to work as a peon at a local school. It was there, at the age of nine years old, that Venkat first remembers meeting his uncle Jangarh, who at that time was enrolled in a government-run vocational training programme. Venkat recalls that he and his younger brother Beeran would spend many mornings swimming and fishing in the nearby Narmada River, and that at the end of the day Jangarh would return from work with wood shavings sufficient for them to cook their freshly caught fish. At that time they prided themselves on being self-reliant, doing everything from fashioning their own iron plough to giving one another haircuts. In 1981 Jangarh returned to Patangarh where he was "discovered" by Swaminathan's talent scouts; meanwhile, Venkat and his father resettled, along with his mother and the rest of the family, first in the village of Jeharmau and then, after a year, back in Sijhora. In both places Pyare Lal continued working as a peon in local schools. Venkat attended local classes in an intermittent, informal way, until his father teased him about having fallen many classes behind other students. Venkat became so angry that he left home vowing never to return, and moved into a Christian friend's home in Sijhora. He supported himself first by stitching shirts and trousers (at Rs 1 per item), digging ditches and cutting *lantana* weeds for a government food-for-work programme, and eventually supervising other labourers (for which his monthly compensation was a quintal of wheat, three and a half kilograms of rapeseed oil and Rs 250).

At that time (in 1986), his uncle Jangarh—accompanied by his mother, wife and year-old son—briefly came from Bhopal to visit the family in Sijhora. Jangarh had recently won the state's "Shikhar Samman" (Summit Award) for his art; meanwhile, Venkat's own artistic efforts were then limited to sketches in pencil or coal—the latter, according to Venkat, being traditionally considered inauspicious and thus the cause of chastisements—in which he emulated the "realistic" renderings of film stars drawn by his late uncle Jawahar[87] after magazine and newspaper illustrations. Jangarh saw Venkat's drawings and encouraged him to come work as an artist in Bhopal. Initially Venkat was reluctant, but then he agreed to join him, and lived at Jangarh's home in Professors Colony while working as his painting apprentice for a couple years. Venkat also did his own artworks, for which he developed a distinctive figural style, featuring broader bands of diagonal shading divided by narrow black-and-white striped bands, patterns he calls *lahr* and *lahrdaar*

Venkat Raman Singh Shyam and his wife Saroj, at their home in Bhopal, 2002.

("choppy waves" and "smooth waves"; see Figs. 17, 20 and 21). For his paintings in colour he uses a motif he calls *chakmak* ("flint stone"—in reference to the primordial spark of fire, life and creativity; e.g., as shown in the lower purple areas of Fig. 19). To generate further income, Venkat also started painting sign boards (for Rs 45-50 a day). An altercation with Jangarh's mother prompted him to move to Delhi, where he survived by doing various jobs—ranging from domestic housework and house painting, to plying a rickshaw and working as an electrician, plumber and mason. A relative introduced him to J. Swaminathan, whose studio Venkat often visited, and for whom he helped arrange the wedding reception for Swaminathan's younger son. It was there that Swaminathan introduced Venkat to such leading Indian musicians and artists as Hariprasad Chaurasia, Ravi Shankar and Manjit Bawa. Thereafter Jangarh visited Delhi and again offered to help Venkat sell his paintings.

A serious bout of bad health and loss from a theft in 1993 forced Venkat to leave Delhi, first for Bhopal and then Sijhora. After recovering in his father's home in the village, he was pressured into an arranged marriage. Shortly thereafter he returned alone to Bhopal, where he resumed work as a signboard painter for Shree Advertising. Meanwhile, back at the village his newly wed wife unexpectedly passed away, occasioning his return for the funeral. After some difficult interactions with his in-laws, he decided to return to Bhopal, and soon remarried—this time to Saroj, a seventeen-year-old Gond girl.

Throughout these vicissitudes, Venkat continued working on his own paintings, and in 1998 joined Bhajju Shyam on a trip to Pondicherry to meet Hervé Perdriolle of the Outsider Art Gallery, to whom Venkat sold five paintings for Rs 500 each—for him an unprecedented sum. Other opportunities followed: he attended an artists' workshop sponsored by the Development Commissioner for Handicrafts in Delhi, where he met designers who commissioned him to produce greeting cards for Khajuraho's 2000 millennium celebrations, and arranged to exhibit his work at the US Embassy in Delhi. Venkat also sold works through the Madhya Pradesh Hastashilp Vikas Nigam (Handicrafts Development Corporation), and was invited to show his work at art galleries in Delhi and Mumbai, where his paintings were included in a group exhibit—entitled "Anaadi"—organized by the artist Akhilesh, curated by the Bengali art critic Rattanotama Sen Gupta, and held at Mumbai's National Gallery of Modern Art in 2001. Meanwhile he continued to depend on painting signboards to support himself and his young family (by then his wife Saroj had given birth to two children)—until he learned of Jangarh's suicide in Japan. Reflecting on Jangarh's death, Venkat vowed to stop painting signboards and instead follow his mentor's example and dedicate himself solely to his own creative artwork. While working on a Republic Day Celebration commission for Bhopal's Adivasi Lok Kala Parishad (Tribal People's Art Council), Venkat encountered Dhananjay Pimpalkhute, a contemporary (non-tribal) Bhopal-based artist; they later collaborated on a series of art commissions for hotels operated by the Madhya Pradesh Tourist Corporation. This work was done in a variety of media: *papier maché*, ceramic tiles, acrylic and oil paintings on canvas, glass, aluminum and iron sheets.[88] In 2004, on behalf of a Scottish company called West Highland Animation, Venkat organized an impromptu team of fellow Gond artists to produce cel imagery (rendered in the distinctive Gondi style first invented by Jangarh) for a televised episode of an animated film for children, based on a traditional Gond story (see Fig.40). Since then, Venkat has become a board member of Dastkari Haat Samiti (Crafts Market Association, a Delhi-based non-profit organization dedicated to promoting and marketing traditional Indian arts and crafts), while continuing to do special commissions and selling his own paintings through displays and exhibitions both nationally and abroad.[89] Most recently, Venkat visited Mumbai to deliver artworks to the city's Taj Hotel on November 27, 2008—the very day the hotel was attacked by terrorists.[90] After witnessing the attack, Venkat decided to add this personal experience of globalized terrorism to his ever-expanding repertoire of subject matter; in April 2009, his series of sixteen paintings depicting the attack was shown in a solo exhibit at Bhopal's Indira Gandhi National Museum of Mankind.

The Challenges of Cultural Adaptation and Survival

Venkat's experimentation with various subject matter, media, styles and marketing approaches offers a vivid example of the eager, flexible attitude with which some contemporary Gond artists pursue new means of self-expression and patronage. Illustrated children's books and a multi-lingual international animated film may seem far removed from this art movement's humble beginnings of domestic reliefs, murals and *digna* designs in Patangarh, and it remains to be seen just how much further these artists can innovate while maintaining viable ties with their tribal traditions and identity. Still, it must be remembered that for centuries the Pardhan Gonds sustained themselves as itinerant performers accepting payments from far-flung patrons, and so the commercial aspect of their recent visual expression through modern media can be seen as an innovative revival of—rather than a simple departure from—their community's traditional pursuits. Now the Pardhan Gonds' narrative talents are being increasingly channeled, encouraged and rewarded with experimental collaborations, commissions and expanded forms of patronage—resulting in varying degrees of commercial and aesthetic success. Mass-produced Gond pictures are churned out for the tourist and ethnic arts markets, and some Gond artists have also branched into hand-painting decorative hangings, pillow covers, purses, furniture, puppets, stuffed animals and toys. Much of this output is intended to appeal to a broad-spread

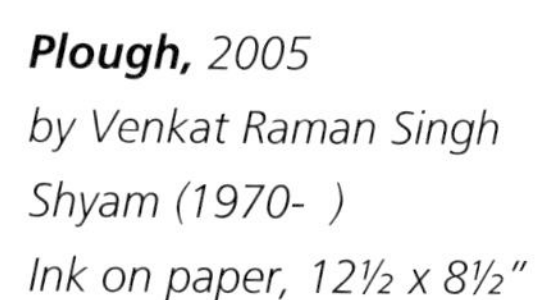

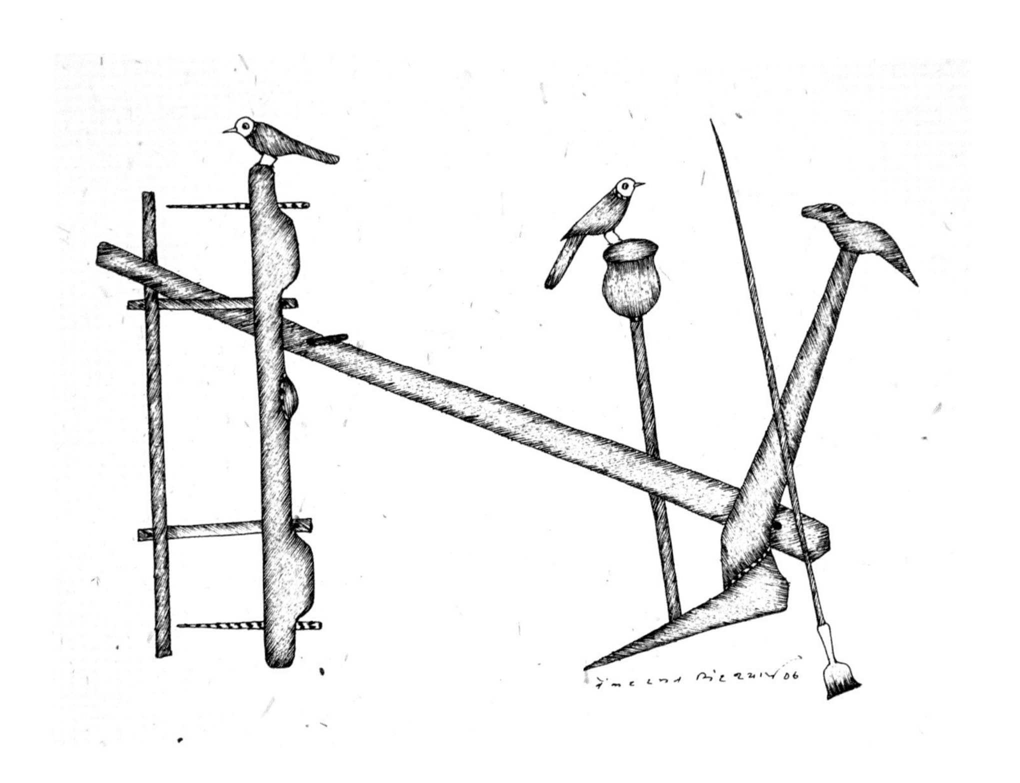

Plough, *2005*
by Venkat Raman Singh Shyam (1970-)
Ink on paper, 12½ x 8½"

Left to right: Mid-20th century Patangarh mural of demons (photographed by Verrier Elwin); and 1996 depiction of demons by Ram Singh Urveti, Acrylic and ink on canvas 34½ x 4½" (see page 55 for the artist's account of this subject).

yet belittling preconception that contemporary tribal artists are best able to produce charmingly decorative or child-oriented imagery. The prominent use of Gond artistic talents for illustrating children's books and animated films—largely based on non-traditional (and sometimes pseudo-traditional) story lines developed by non-tribals—is problematic. The extent to which outside customers' and patrons' tastes and preferences can also influence these arts has been indicated by two of the styles practiced by Suresh Singh Dhurvey—one which he does for clients wanting something "tribal", the other a more "acculturated" style, pursued mostly for his own personal satisfaction. Yet, as also shown in this essay, Suresh feels personally committed to perpetuating a "tribal" art style too, both in his own work and that of his children. While "strategic positioning" and pandering for profit are (and always have been) lucrative temptations for *all* professional artists, obviously marginalized tribal artists—who have only recently risen from extreme poverty—are particularly vulnerable. And, of course, exploitation can happen both abroad and closer to home too, as Gond artists have not yet fully learned how (or simply cannot afford) to limit sales of their work to established galleries—which in turn do not always extend the same sort of professional treatment to tribal artists that they show towards other, better-educated urban artists. Gond artists are otherwise limited to marketing their work through arts and crafts fairs, and occasional special commissions and direct sales to rare patrons particularly interested in the genre. But that may soon begin to change, as Bhajju Shyam, Venkat Raman Singh Shyam and other leading Gond artists gradually become more savvy about Indian and foreign art dealers and galleries. Other influential factors include the involvement of both government and non-government agencies sponsoring regular tribal art awards,[91] promoting an alien and non-traditional competitive factor into Gond creativity. One can but wonder how such modern dynamics will affect these artists' relations with one another, and the creation and assessment of their artwork itself.

The number and magnitude of the cultural transitions this community of talented tribals has made over the past decades—moving from isolated villages to Bhopal and establishing themselves in relation to unfamiliar economies, as well as new social environments, institutions, professions and lifestyles—can hardly be grasped by those of us born into urban modernity. They have shown remarkable solidarity and willingness to assist and collaborate with one another. It must also be said that ongoing financial pressures have gradually generated a fair measure of polite, competitive rivalry. While Jangarh was alive he served as a kind of benevolent patriarch, ever-eager to minimize frictions and promote both the interests of individual Gond artists and their struggling community as a whole. His death caused great anguish and a deep sense of insecurity; but—with time and further successes on their own—the Bhopal-based Gond artists have demonstrated their resilience and renewed commitment to their vocation, and now many of their children are also starting to pursue art careers of their own too. Jangarh was born in 1960; his successors exhibited here were born in the early 1970s, and now a new generation of their offspring—born in Bhopal—is coming of age to face similar but somewhat different challenges, for which there are no easy well-established formulas to follow.

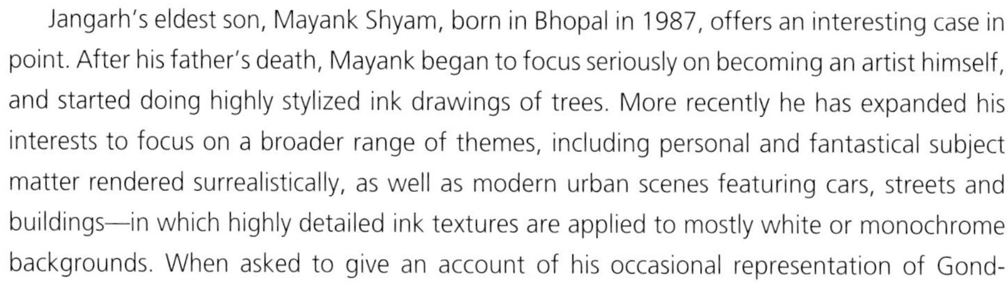

Jangarh's eldest son, Mayank Shyam, born in Bhopal in 1987, offers an interesting case in point. After his father's death, Mayank began to focus seriously on becoming an artist himself, and started doing highly stylized ink drawings of trees. More recently he has expanded his interests to focus on a broader range of themes, including personal and fantastical subject matter rendered surrealistically, as well as modern urban scenes featuring cars, streets and buildings—in which highly detailed ink textures are applied to mostly white or monochrome backgrounds. When asked to give an account of his occasional representation of Gond-specific subject matter—as in the case of his ink drawing of a *sanpharki* (a fabled yet much-feared winged snake whose shadow purportedly causes paralysis, [see right page])—Mayank has relatively little to say compared to village-born artists. On the other hand, he has a fertile imagination and greatly enjoys writing his own romantic stories and poetry. While Mayank is clearly very gifted, it remains to be seen whether he decides to delve more meaningfully and deeply into his tribal heritage as a *Gond* artist, or instead use his distinctive style to explore non-Gond-specific subject matter—and thus establish himself in the "art world" either as an "Outsider" artist,[92] or simply as a contemporary artist who just happens to be Gond.

Mayank Shyam at his family home at Professors Colony, Bhopal, 2007. He holds his unfinished pen and ink drawing— ***Memories of Jangarh Singh Shyam****—beneath his father Jangarh's framed photograph and drawing*

As Jangarh's eldest son, Mayank clearly has certain advantages in establishing himself in the contemporary urban art world.[93] Yet his family's prominence also entails certain responsibilities: he may increasingly be expected to serve as a kind of Gond cultural ambassador to the outside world. One of his recent and ambitious artworks is a drawing—entitled *Memories of Jangarh Singh Shyam* (here shown in the process of being completed, at left)—in which Mayank symbolically represents his late father's life, creativity and influence on the larger community of Gond artists. Many well-wishers of Jangarh's family are eager (if not indeed a bit anxious) to see if and how Mayank may become a trail blazer like his father, and thereby provide a role model to his generation of young Gond artists—either by re-engaging with his people's rich traditions, or by forging on in a more individualistic way, less focused on his tribal heritage.

The older generation of artists represented in this publication have children and are concerned about their education, career prospects and future Pardhan Gond identity. Suresh Singh Dhurvey's reflections may be seen as representative:

Sanpharki
2002
by Mayank Shyam
(1987-)
Pen and ink drawing

> "I have one son and two daughters. My ten-year-old daughter Sharda is the eldest, and she is interested in painting. She had participated in the painting camp at the Swaraj Bhawan at Bhopal. I tell my daughter that she should now concentrate on her studies, because I do not want her to be deprived of education such as I was; I very much want my children to excel in society, and not face the hardships and difficulties that I have faced and continue to face—from a lack of education. [...] All the children of the Gond painters of Bhopal do painting work. Jangarh used to tell his son Mayank that he should concentrate on his studies, but now Mayank—after finishing the tenth standard at school—has completely left his studies to do art. Since most of these children are not exposed to the village life, they tend to paint urban themes – like palaces, mosques or temples and modern buildings. I don't know if they're able to sell these paintings. Jangarh used to tell Mayank that he should study so that he could at least talk to outsiders properly. Therefore, I tell my children that they too must concentrate on their studies. And in so far as learning art is concerned they're always exposed to that at home anyway, because I'm always there doing my artwork. My intention is that I would expose them to [traditional Gond] stories, myths and beliefs as they mature. And I'm confident that they'll be able to absorb it all. I'm also conscious of the fact that if the children remain merely exposed to the urban environment, their painting style will drift from the tribal style of painting. But I'm confident that my children will absorb the stories and beliefs I tell them, and so their style will be in keeping with the tribal style. Every year I take my family to Patangarh and stay there for a full month—usually in March-April, when it's somewhat cooler there than in Bhopal. In the sunshine it's hot, but inside it stays tolerably cool, and there are breezes. That's also the wedding season, when no fieldwork is being done. So my children get much opportunity to interact with their family and others there, hear stories told and learn Gond customs."[94]

Over a half-century ago, the first book written by a native Indian and devoted solely to Pardhan Gond culture wistfully concluded with the hope of finding some means for its continued survival. Perhaps the images and iconographies now presented in this exhibition and publication will serve as a positive if partial fulfillment of Shamrao Hivale's closing lines:

> "There must surely be some means whereby the riches of the ancient life can be carried over into the conditions of the modern world. For if ever a world will need poetry, it will be the world of tomorrow." [95]

CATALOGUE

Fig. 1.
The Friendship of the Tiger and the Boar [96]
1989
by Jangarh Singh Shyam
(1960-2001)
Acrylics on canvas
43½ x 31½"

Very few detailed iconographic explanations by Jangarh Singh Shyam were recorded directly from him during his lifetime. Fortunately, he briefly explained this painting in 1998. The following account is paraphrased from notes taken at that time.

The painting shows a time at the beginning of the world when mankind was still undifferentiated from all the other animals, living without clothes or civilization. In the tree can be seen both a man and two monkeys, the only difference shown between them here being the man's lack of a tail. The picture has been divided into three separate realms: *akaash* [the sky], *dharti* [the earth's surface] and *patal* [the underworld]. In the painting's lower left quadrant appear the tiger and the boar, who were great friends in the first of times. But then the boar had children, and they expressed much fear of the tiger, and thus the boar felt compelled to distance herself from her old friend. This painting shows the tiger trying to pacify the boar's anxieties, reminiscing over the happy times they shared in the past—but the boar replies that she must now keep at a distance, with her children. There is a traditional Gond song about this poignant moment of parting friendship. [JHB & SS]

Among the Pardhan Gonds of eastern Madhya Pradesh, as elsewhere in rural India, the image of a scorpion is generally considered auspicious. Jangarh's large tinted drawing is unusually elaborate. Its body is covered with fantastically swirling linear patterns—which have more to do with the power to mesmerize than capturing naturalistic appearances. The tail section, comprised of interlaced leaf-like designs, is rendered with an almost Edo Japanese elegance. Here Jangarh combines the application of washes of colour with superimposed stenciling, in which the paint is speckled onto the paper from the stroked bristles of a toothbrush.

Fig. 2. ***Scorpion***[97], 1993
by Jangarh Singh Shyam
(1960-2001)
Ink and watercolours on paper
20 x 26¼"

At right is one of two identical clay reliefs flanking the front door of the home of Santosh Paraste, Jangarh's next-door neighbor in Patangarh. The addition of two eyes transforms a scorpion's body into the visage of the elephant-headed god Ganesh (rendered with attention to iconographic details such as one complete and one broken tusk, as well the sign of a Shivite *tirshul* [trident] on his forehead). Thus two auspicious images—both traditionally associated with entry doors—are merged into one composite vision. Similar ingeniously composite imagery recurs throughout contemporary Pardhan Gond paintings, and elsewhere in Indian art. [JHB]

Fig. 3.
Owl
1997
by Jangarh Singh Shyam
(1960-2001)
Acrylic and ink on canvas
34½ x 24¼"

Fig. 4.
Owl
1999
by Subhash Vyam (1970-)
Wood sculpture
15 x 12½ x 4½"

In the above painting, Jangarh Singh Shyam boldly experimented with different kinds of jazzy black-and-white patterns. The entire figure is surrounded by a nimbus of fine radiating lines, which Jangarh often used to suggest power and/or movement. He later added an outer pale yellow overlay of paint and surrounding black border, to magnify the figure's overall startling impact. The owl is considered an inauspicious bird. [JHB]

According to the sculptor Subhash Vyam:

"Whenever the owl speaks upon the roofs of the houses it tries to say things about the family members—to alert them about approaching problems—so they can avoid them, by *puja* [worship] or by consulting a *gunia* [tribal priest with healing powers]. But whenever a person throws a stone at an owl, the owl gets that stone and dips it into the river, takes it back onto the riverbank, and there lets it dry. As it dries the person who threw it gets weaker and weaker; the owl does this repeatedly—until, after a few days, the person dies. Thus the owl takes its revenge." [DU]

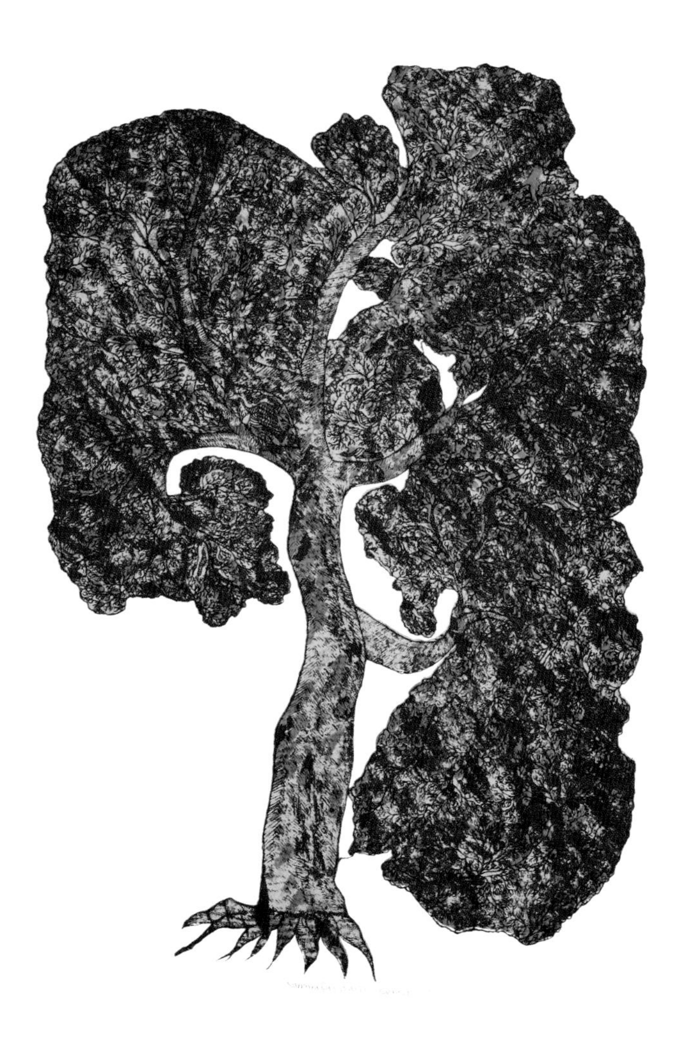

Fig. 5.
Harada Tree
1987
by Jangarh Singh Shyam
(1960-2001)
Silkscreen on paper
24½ x 16¼"

The *harada* tree (a.k.a. "purple leaf plum"[98]) is indigenous to the Indian subcontinent and provides one of the three key ingredients for the herbal/Ayurvedic medicine *triphala* (lit.: "three fruits"), commonly used (by tribals and non-tribals alike) as an aid to digestion and to cure constipation.

According to Jangarh's nephew, the artist Venkat Raman Singh Shyam, the *harada* is traditionally considered to be inhabited by a demonic deity, who appears in its leaves as a flame and/or ghosts, and is also perceived as movements of the tree's leaves and branches. Venkat further said that he witnessed Jangarh develop such compositions out of the inadvertent watermarks left by wet items placed on paper. This combined inspiration accounts for both the strange twistings of the tree's branches and leaves, and the rather sinister claw-like forms of its roots. Also noteworthy are detailed representations of branches, twigs and numerous tiny birds within the tree's leafy areas, as well as Jangarh's alternating placement of emerald green bands of colour in a subtle counterclockwise swirl to convey a sense of movement. The silkscreen medium has rarely been used to create such rich effects, thus making this print a connoisseur's delight.[99] [JHB]

The Creation of the Earth is a favorite Pardhan Gond myth. It was first recorded in the early 20th century,[100] **and has been told and depicted in various ways. Here four artists have interpreted in their distinctive styles different scenes from the myth, while a translation of one artist's account gives the basic story.** [JHB]

Fig. 6.
Brahma-ji[101]
1995
by Jangarh Singh Shyam
(1960-2001)
Ink on canvas
43½ x 18½"[102]

According to the artist Venkat Raman Singh Shyam:

"For ages Bara Deo [Great God] lay in a deep slumber upon the *purain paan* [lotus leaf] and nothing happened. Finally he woke up, rubbed a little dirt from his body with which he created a white bird. He ordered the bird to go in search of the earth. The bird kept flying for three days and nights, and then came across a hooded snake peeping out of the waters. The tired bird sat on it without asking permission and was turned black due to the poisonous breath of Shesh Nag [the hooded snake], and thus the bird came to be known as Kaag Bhusund [Crow, the Black One]. The bird flew from there and then came across a crab's claw jutting out from the surface of the water. After listening to the crow, the crab took him down below the waters to Kichukmal Raja [Earthworm King] and his queen, who then had the earth all to themselves. The king and queen did not want to part with the earth and so the queen started hastily swallowing it. The crab pressed her neck and she spat earth. The crow made earth into a ball and, holding it in his beak, flew back. The way to Bara Deo was long and, to the crow's dismay, he dropped the earth ball which fell into the Kingdom of Mailagarh [the Dirt Kingdom]. The bird returned to Bara Deo and reported what happened, and Bara Deo asked Vishnu to do something about it. Vishnu took the incarnation of a boar—as a boar is not bothered by the dirt and even consumes it, and also has immense power—and brought back the earth to Bara Deo. After churning the earth, he smeared it over the lotus leaf and waters. The Jalharin Mata [the Goddess Insect, who lives under water] was grieved, because she was then plunged into darkness. Being a *bigadna* [a 'spoilsport' who undoes whatever is done], she bored through the not-yet-dried earth, and it fell apart in small pieces. The next morning Bara Deo found clay lumps floating over the water's surface, which he again gathered and re-smeared on the surface of the lotus leaf and waters. That night he kept watch, and was able to catch Jalharin Mata and threw her high into the air. She came down whirling and turned into a *ghongha* [a conch snail], which is her form to this day. This is how the earth was created.

"Depicted here in the centre of the painting is the lotus leaf upon which rests Bara Deo surrounded by waters; the wavy earthworm-like forms denote water, as well as the scattered clay lumps floating on the water. The bird Kaag Bhusund is also shown." [SS]

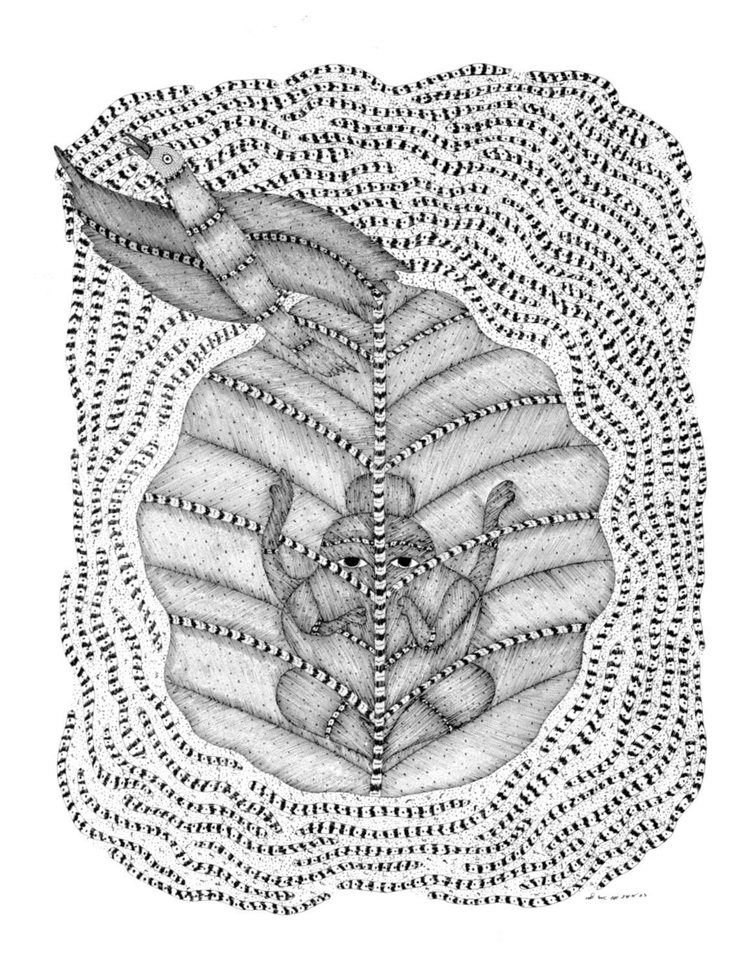

Fig. 7.
The Story of Creation
2003
by Venkat Raman Singh Shyam (1970-)
Ink and watercolours on paper
24½ x 19½"

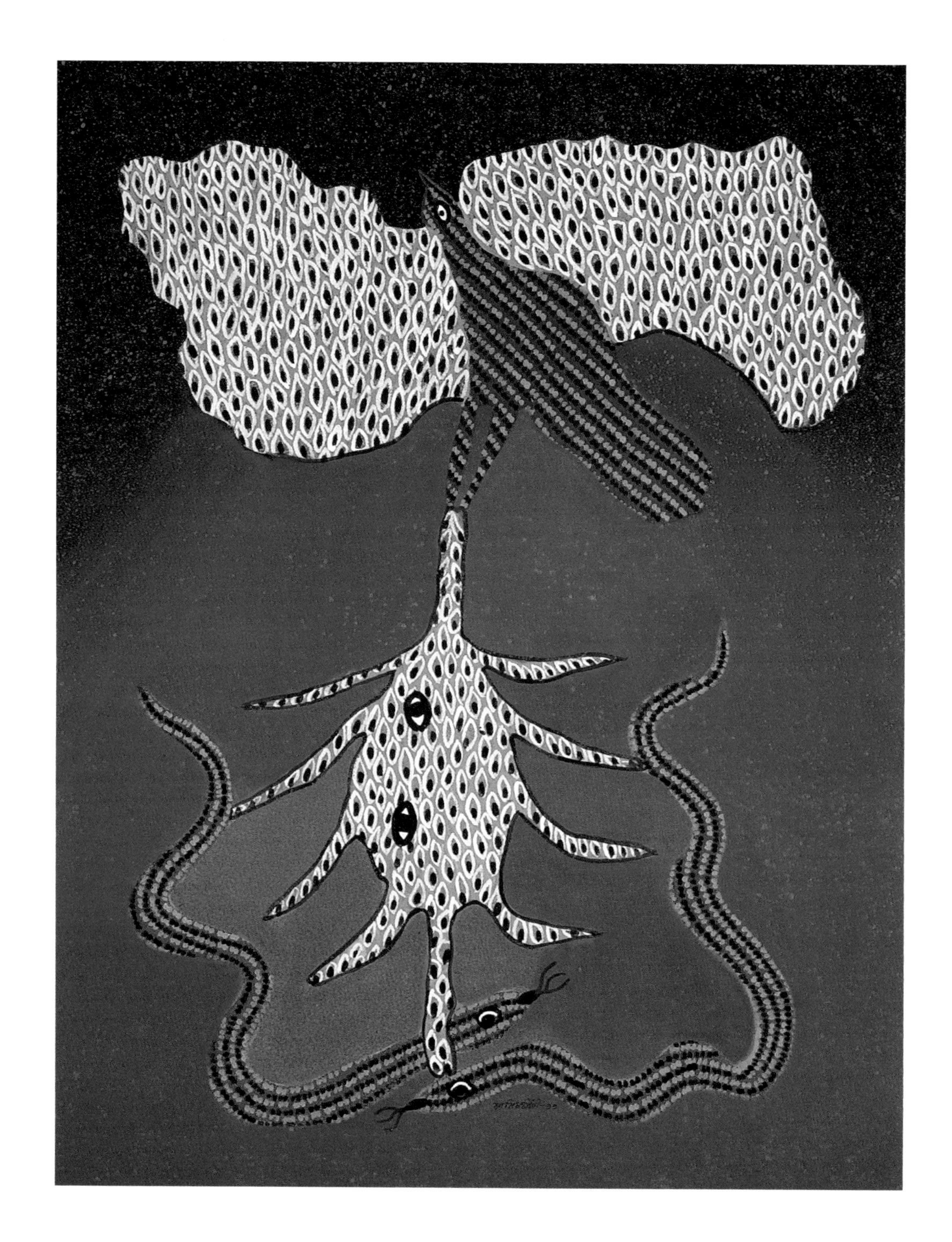

Fig. 8.
Creation of the Earth
1999
by Ram Singh Urveti (1965-)
Acrylic on canvas , 30¼ x 27½"

Fig. 9. (right page)
Kaag Bhusund Alights on Nag Devita
2007
by Bhajju Shyam (1971-)
Acrylic on canvas, 48 x 40½"

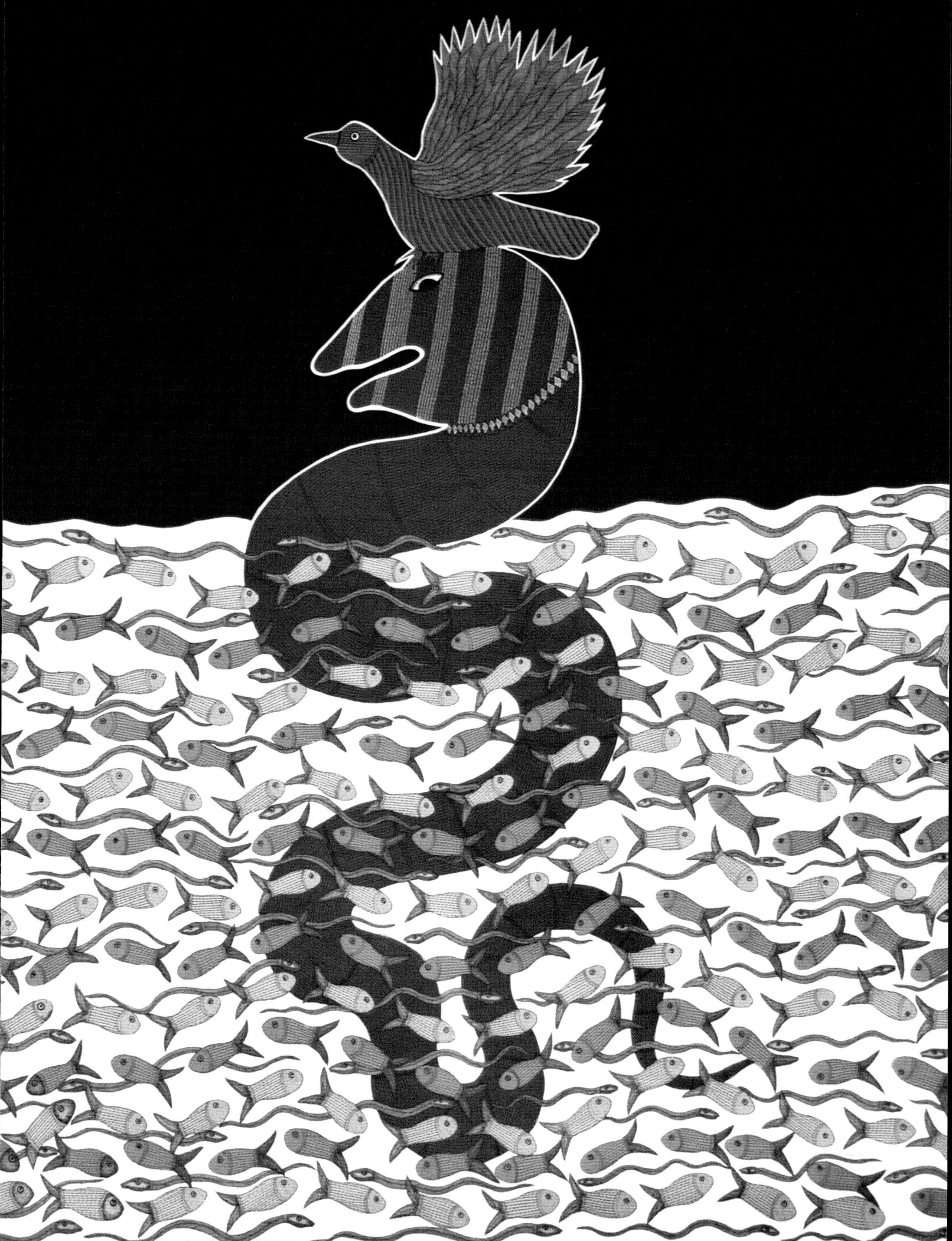

Fig. 10.
Raja Heera Khan Chhatri and the Demon Son Bara
2006
by Bhajju Shyam
(1971-)
Acrylic and ink on canvas
46½" x 36"

According to the artist:

"There was a tribal king by the name of Raja Herra Khan Chhatri, whose kingdom was afflicted by a demon that had assumed the form of a terrible pig named Son Bara. This demon pig lived on the kingdom's borders and would challenge to combat all those who tried to enter it. Raja Herra Khan Chhatri rode a powerful flying horse, itself the incarnation of a god, and in whose body resided goddesses who embodied different forms of *shakti* [energy]; some resided in the horse's wings, others in its legs and neck, and also in its head. In order to vanquish the demon pig, two of these goddesses entered his body through his mouth and built a fire in his stomach. Thus all the *buri shakti*s [bad energies] within Son Bara were flushed out of his mouth and ears, the fire consumed him—and peace was restored to Raja Herra Khan Chhatri's kingdom. I have shown one of the evacuated bad energies seated in the lower right corner." [ID]

Gond oral history and mythology celebrate the heroic deeds of several great *raja*s and *rani*s (kings and queens). Some of these monarchs are based on actual historical rulers of three medieval Gond dynastic kingdoms, while others—such as Raja Heera Khan Chhatri—are clearly fabulous inventions.[103] To this day, the Pardhans' recounting of these royal exploits serves as a source of entertainment and pride for Gond tribals throughout central India. [JHB]

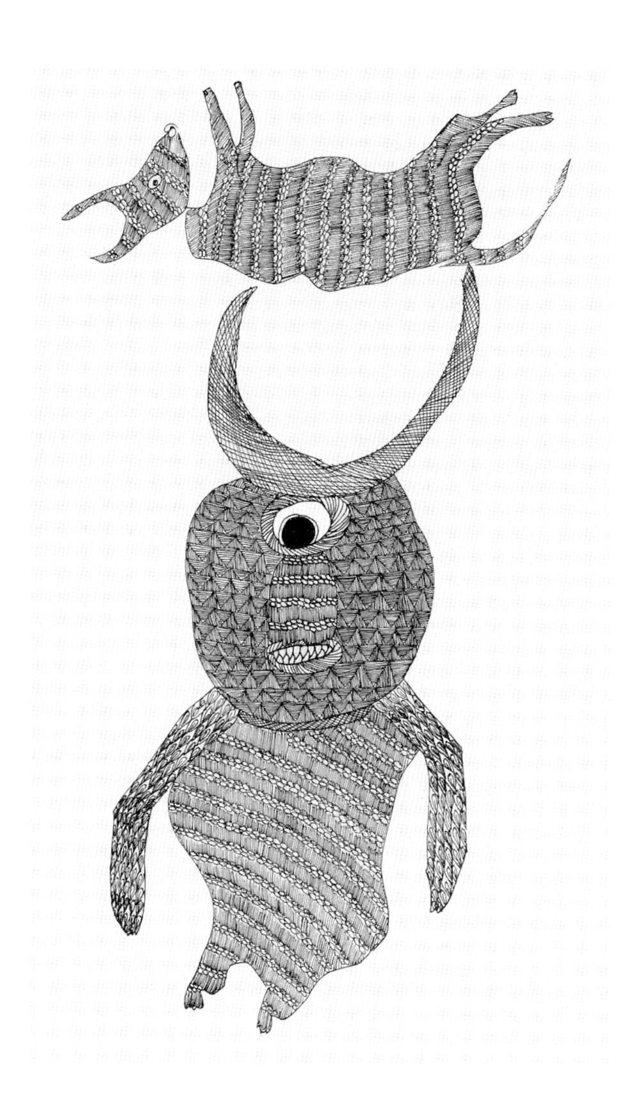

According to the artist:

"Duda Rakas and Duda Raksin [the Duda Demon and Demoness] were terrorizing the villagers so much that they did the *puja* of the Adi Shakti [Goddess of Primordial Energy] to ask that she kill them. The Adi Shakti took three forms: that of a human, a horse and a boar. Only in the form of the boar was Adi Shakti successful in vanquishing them into the jungle, where they still live by preying on wild animals. These pictures show Duda Rakas [the Cyclops] and Duda Raksin [shown with two eyes], each carrying a carcass of wild game from the jungle for their daily food.

"In our tradition, the worship of the Adi Shakti comes from this story. Thereafter the Adi Shakti became known as Narayan Dev [an incarnation of Vishnu]. That is because the Shakti took the form of the boar [as did Vishnu in his Varaha incarnation]. When Narayan Dev is worshipped at home, we offer the boar as a sacrifice, and feast upon it thereafter." [ID]

Figs. 11 a & b.
Duda Rakas and Duda Raksin
1999
by Ram Singh Urveti
(1965-)
Ink on paper
Duda Rakas (left)
19 x 10½"
Duda Raksin (right)
19½ x 12"

Fig. 12.
Mangrohi
2007
by Ram Singh Urveti
(1965-)
Ink on canvas
47¼ x 40½"

According to the artist:

"For marriage a *mandap* [a canopied space where the marriage ceremonies are conducted] is made of wood, branches and leaves from the *doomar* [a.k.a. *goolar*] tree.[104] The *mangrohi* is the *mandap*'s free-standing central post. *Doomar* wood can be combined with various other woods for constructing the *mandap's* upright structure, but only the *doomar* should be used for the *mangrohi* and the overhead leafy canopy. The *mangrohi* is not made by everyone, but rather by a knowledgeable person called the *gunia*. Every *gunia* makes a *mangrohi* face according to his wish. The *gunia* chants certain mantras at the time when the *mangrohi* is first fixed into the earth, so as to protect the newlyweds from dangers. I myself have never actually made a *mangrohi,* but I know how it is done. One first makes a clean post from the stump of a *doomar* tree, into which are affixed the leafy branches of the *doomar*, *baans* [bamboo] and *saja* ["crocodile-bark tree"].[105] I have shown *doomar* leaves as the small black dots throughout the painting. Charcoal and turmeric designs are applied to the *mangrohi* post to depict the face of the household's primary deity. At the bottom I have shown a *kalash* [pot] upon which a *dipa* [oil lamp] has been set and lit for ceremonies held throughout the day and night; it must burn at night, but it is not so important that it must constantly burn during the day. In the pot they normally put coins and grain—but I've not shown that. The number of branches projecting out of the *mangrohi* could be any number—here I've shown eight. Within the circles [at bottom right and left] I've shown two pieces of *doomar*—called *chanti*—which are used for clapping together at the time of dance. They are shown beneath a couple of mango leaves, which are first dipped into a pot of oil and then taken to the forehead of the god and brought down the entire length of the post a total of seven times. We believe that by doing so the marriage will survive for seven births. That is also why the *mangrohi* is circumambulated seven times. Above the *chanti* and mango leaves I've shown the *jhanpi*, which is a circular bamboo basket with a lid on top, into which the bride's family put gifts for the groom, and the groom's family put their gifts for the bride. The *mandap* is set up in both the boy's and the girl's respective family courtyards. Four circumambulations are made around the boy's family *mangrohi,* and three around the girl's family *mangrohi*. In the circles above I have shown both the *lodha* and the *siloti* [the flat and cylindrical pieces of stone used mainly for grinding grain], here used for grinding turmeric into the paste smeared on the boy and girl at the time of their ritual bath. All these things are kept in the *mandap* at the time of wedding ceremonies. In upper right circle I've shown the bride, and in the upper left circle the groom.

"Normally I don't sketch; I paint directly. I do all my painting directly—I've never touched a pencil. Actually, this is an ink drawing on canvas, not a painting. In drawing I use a garland or a leaf as the design motif. The central figure here is made with the leaf motif, the twisted garland [pattern] is seen here on the bride and groom. On the bottom pot I've used the *digna* motif—an auspicious zig-zag pattern—which I've filled in with my *mala* [necklace] motif, which is here made up out of [alternating triangles of] vertical and horizontal lines. It is difficult to use the *mala* and leaf patterns in a painting." [ID]

Gond **mangrohi**
mid-20th century
photo by Verrier Elwin.[106]

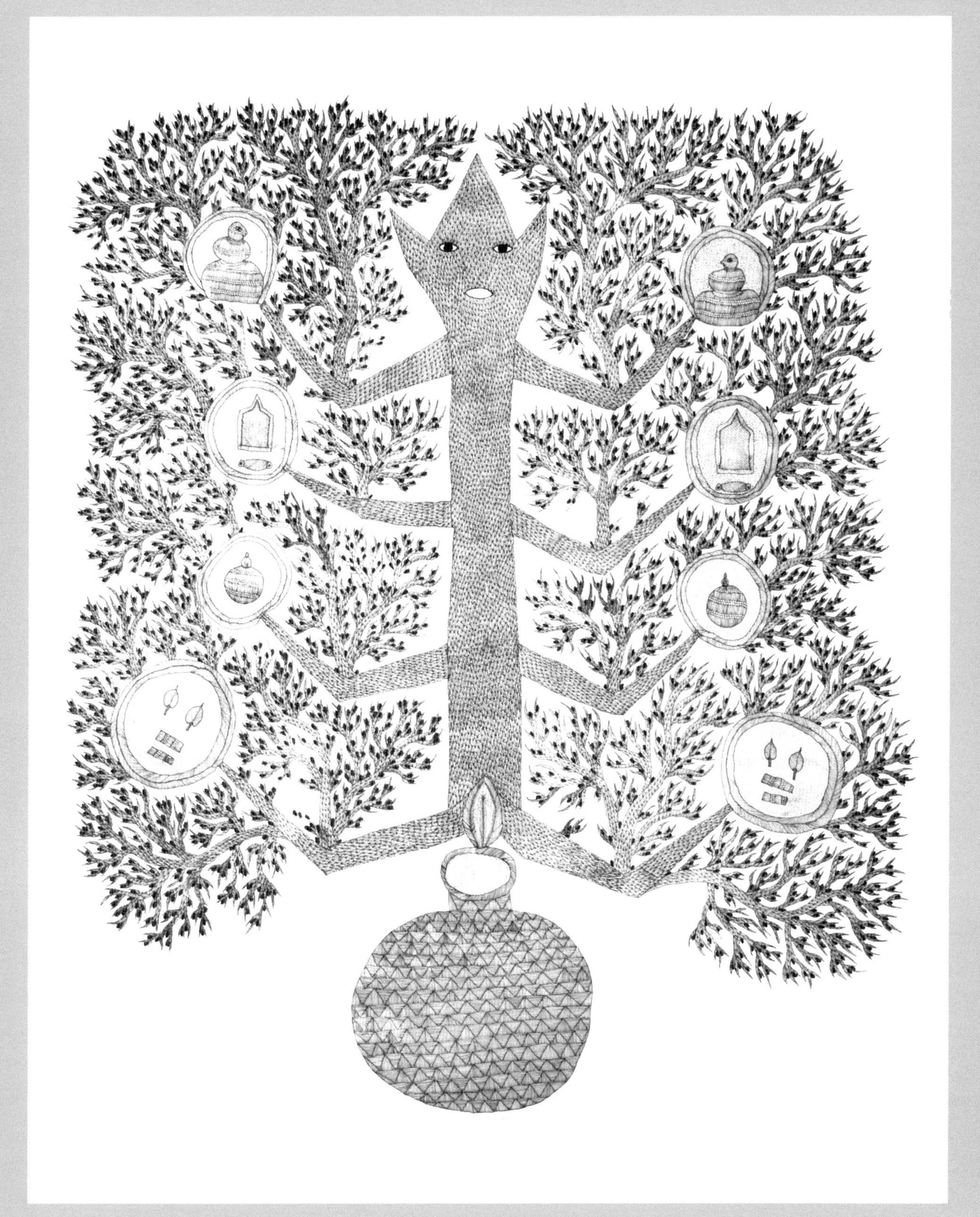

Fig. 13.

The Karma Song of the Gond Tribals
2004
by Ram Singh Urveti
(1965-)
Acrylic on canvas
41 x 73"

According to the artist:

"The Karma is a song of joy performed on joyous occasions, such as when guests visit one's household, at weddings, or on the occasions of festivals, such as the Madai Mela [the Madai Fair]. It may be accompanied by dance, but that is not essential. On the left of this picture is shown a *lomri* [fox] playing the *tabla* [upright drums], and above him two people are listening. On the far right is a *kharkhire* [civet], which burrows its holes in paddy fields—and is here shown sowing a paddy field. Before him [shown as yellow form] is a *mandar* drum that's played during the sowing, and above him is a *bhaloo* [bear], who carries on his head a basket full of field grass, which he is about to throw into a garbage pit. A partridge [coloured red] and a *lava* [quail, coloured blue] are shown plowing the field with the help of a pair of bullocks. Two monkeys are also shown playing on the *manjira* [cymbals]. Birds are flying about over the fields, and some of them are eating the freshly sowed paddy seeds. The Karma song shown in this picture goes:

The fox is playing on the tabla, *by using his hands on the surface of the* tabla,
The monkey plays on the manjira,
The partridge and the quail are plowing the field,
The civet is sowing the paddy seed.
The clay manjira *is taking the pair of bullocks for grazing,*
And the bear is taking the grass in a basket on his head to throw away.

"I like this song's rhyme and melody, and since I paint animals and trees in my work, I chose the song as the subject of this painting. There are many other very sweet Karma Songs. Those who perform these songs like to show others how well they can sing, and so there are singing competitions in which the village audiences voice their appreciation about those who sing especially well. Such songs are performed by those who have a flair for singing, but the audience also will join along, in unison. I have it in mind to make similar paintings for other songs as well, but ideas for those have not yet jelled in my mind. For example, I remember when I was ten or twelve years old I used play on the *timki* [a small earthen drum played with small sticks], and someone else would play on the *mandar.* At that time road work was going on, and my maternal uncle was working on the road. At night all the labourers, including the women, would gather around—and one of the women, who came from a neighboring village, sang a song about the sacred river Narmada. And in the song there were references to Lanka and Hanuman of the Ramayana, and other themes—which I've been contemplating how to depict in the form of a painting." [ID]

Karma songs often celebrate love or fertility, and are vigorously sung at joyous occasions. According to the anthropologist Verrier Elwin,[107] the term *karma* refers here both to "fate" and to the *karma* or *karam* tree (*Adina cordifolia,* a flowering deciduous tree), around which special dances are performed. *Karma* songs can be accompanied by various instruments, such as the *bana* (the sacred three-stringed fiddle), *manjira* (cymbals), *chanti* (a wooden clapping instrument), *tabla, timki* and *mandar* (three kinds of drum), and—when accompanied by dance—the stamping of feet and the jangle of women's anklets, toe rings and other ornaments. Many of the songs' lyrics include frequent alliteration, echo words, and onomatopoeic cries. Pardhan Gond paintings likewise feature boldly rhythmic compositions, rich patterns and visual analogies. [JHB]

Fig. 14.
Ganesh/Shiva
1999
by Ram Singh Urveti
(1965-)
Ink on canvas
46½ x 33¼"

Because Ganesh (the elephant-headed god) is the son of Shiva, Ram Singh Urveti thought of combining them into a composite image (shown on facing page). Here each glaring eye of the frontally facing of Shiva can also each be seen as separately associated with either the left- or right-facing Janus-like profile of Ganesh. Each of these profiles features a trunk lifted over a tusk and upwardly raised arm. The artist has used this same distinctive profile configuration elsewhere, such as in his depiction of the infant Ganesh (shown below). Shiva and both profiled Ganeshes ride their respective vehicles: Shiva is mounted on his bull Nandi (shown at bottom, centre); and both profiled depictions of Ganesh ride a rat (shown twice—at bottom right and bottom left; the rats' tails are also shown rising behind them—depicted as the diagonal undulating forms that rise from behind Shiva's hips). According to the artist, the rats are jumping down from the tree which "... for me represents nature in general, and because I come from a place which has jungle all around, so a tree constitutes the most important part of nature." Spade-like forms (shown repeatedly along the central axes of both paintings) depict leaves of the *pipal* (sacred fig tree)[108], and are similar to the leaf-like pendants worn on necklaces in the village.

While the long history of Indian art abounds in images of Ganesh and Shiva, this black and white composite depiction is iconographically and stylistically unprecedented. [JHB & ID]

The Infant Ganesh[109]
1999
by Ram Singh Urveti
Poster paint on paper
13 x 10"

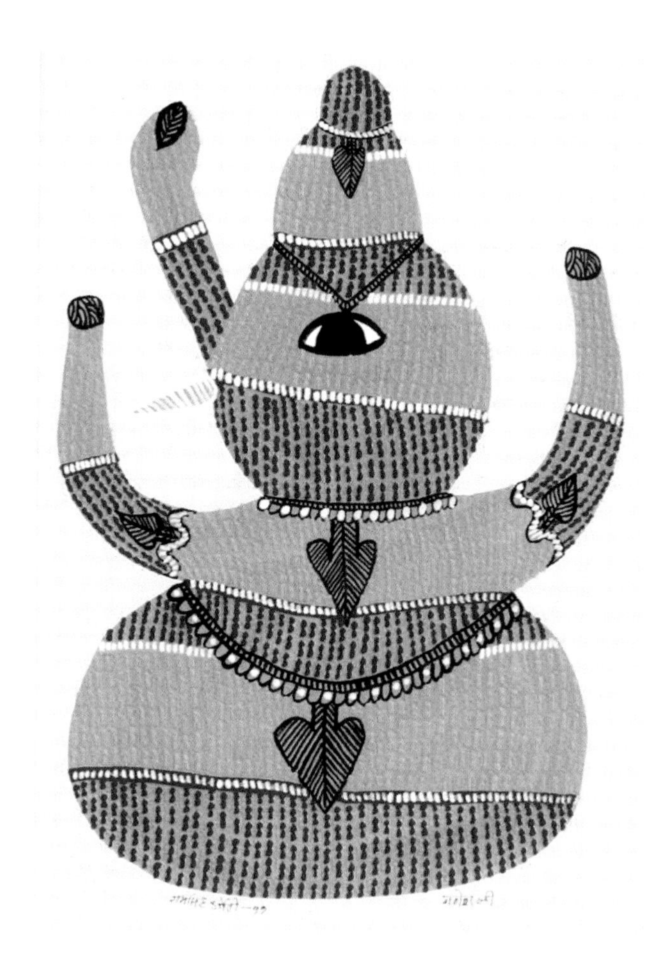

Fig. 15.
Samudra Manthan (The Churning of the Ocean)
2006
by Venkat Raman Singh Shyam
(1970-)
Acrylic and ink on canvas
36¼ x 51"

According to the artist:

"In the primeval times when there was only water and no earth, the universe was ruled by the *surs* and *asurs* [gods and demons]. They used to keep on fighting each other. They then decided to discover something from the ocean which could be equally distributed amongst themselves. They used Himalaya and Shesh Nag [The great snake of Lord Shiva] as a churning staff and rope to churn the ocean—with the gods pulling the rope on one end, and the demons pulling the other. During the process of churning, the first thing that appeared was poison—which I've shown here as the blue colour in the background. Upon seeing this poison, both the gods and demons started running away. They approached Brahma, Vishnu and Shiva—on whose behest they had been churning— and beseeched them to save them from the deadly poison. Brahma said: 'I cannot consume this poison as it is beyond my capacity.' Vishnu said that his Shesh Nag was already being used as a churning rope, and thus he could not do anything. They both suggested that the gods and demons go to Shiva, and that he might be able to help them. Shiva agreed to help, and proposed to use the pipe—which he used for smoking *ganja* [cannabis]—to draw the poison into his body, saying that if he succeeded then it would be good luck for the gods and demons. He then drew the poison and held it in his throat. After that he came to be known as Neelkant ['Blue Throat']. Thereafter the gods and demons started churning the ocean again. Then appeared the *nav ratan* [nine gems], which included the white elephant—which was later named Arawat; Kamdhenu Gai—the cow that eternally yields all necessary things; the horse; then Lakshmi—who when she appeared was taken by Vishnu as his consort; and *amrit*, the elixir of life. These are the gems I know about. All of the *nav ratan* were taken over by the gods. There was a prediction that whosoever tasted the *amrit* would become an immortal. The gods and the demons started arguing over the pot of *amrit*, which the gods took and started running away with it. While they were running, drops of *amrit* fell upon the earth and became sacred places: Allahabad, Ujjain, Nasik and Haridwar. In all these places the Kumbha Mela [a great Hindu religious fair[110]] is held every twelfth year, by rotation. The demons—having lost the *amrit* to the gods—then decided to fight against the gods and thus win rulership of the world.

"After the churning of the ocean, Brahma, Vishnu and Shiva created man and woman, along with the rest of the universe—the plants, animals, and the earth itself.

"Himalaya—which was used as the churning shaft—rested on the Kacchap Raj [King Tortoise]. At the sides of the tortoise shell I've shown its feet in the form of some of the *nav rattan*, which here also indicate the four directions of the earth. The tortoise's head is here represented by the *amrit kalash* [pot of elixir of immortality]. Manu and Shatrupa—the first man and woman—are shown on the earth itself, which I've shown as a tree wherein all sorts of living beings and plants appear. From only one seed everything has emanated, and I've also shown the original seed of creation in the form of the tortoise's tail.

"I've used a broad four-inch wide brush to lightly paint the background colours. Instead of using thickly applied acrylic, I've thinned it out with water to make an atmospheric effect. I've seen other contemporary non-tribal artists use colours in this way, and thus wanted to experiment in a similar way myself. I used washes of cobalt blue, Persian blue, and a bit of crimson red, and a bit of lemon yellow to create the surrounding background effect. In the oval area I used a bit of black, cobalt and Persian blue, yellow, crimson red and a little white. My intent was to make a kind of opal-like effect. Using washes of colour in this way was a new idea for me. I'm pleased by the way it turned out, and am doing more work in this manner."

[ID]

Fig. 16.
Sanpharki
2005
by Venkat Raman Singh Shyam (1970-)
Acrylic on paper
12 x 8½"

According to the artist:

"Any snake, but in particular the king cobra, after reaching its full size slowly starts *decreasing* its size as it approaches the age of one hundred. This decrease takes place because the snake repeatedly sheds its skin. So, by the time it reaches the age of one hundred years old, the king cobra is barely the size of a mouse. At this age the king cobra becomes a *sanpharki*—it sprouts wings and attempts to fly. It doesn't fly at once, but at first hops around—something like a frog. But, after some practice, it finally takes off on its solitary flight. The shadow of a flying *sanpharki* is enough to cause paralysis in anyone upon whom it is cast. At the end of the flight the snake falls down and dies."

The etymology of the name "sanpharki" is worth noting. *Phadki* means to twitch or flap. *San* is a plant whose leaves are used to make ropes, and whose poisonous seeds grow in a shell (like peas in a pod); in Hindi *san* also indicates the sensation and sound of speed. So here the word "sanpharki" is onomatopoeic. [HSB]

The *sanpharki* is unique to Gond tradition, and cannot be found in other Indian mythologies. [JHB]

Fig. 17.
The Flying Elephant
2005
by Venkat Raman Singh Shyam
Ink on canvas
24¼ x 27¾"

According to the artist:

"Many years ago the gods used to travel around from place to place, seated on their mounts. Around that time, the winged white elephant Arawat [the elephant mount of Lord Indra], started roaming around. After a while he started feeling very hungry, and asked his lord permission to search for food on earth. Arawat descended on his wings upon a village, but his weight was such that he crushed the village houses. The villagers were very surprised, for they had never seen such a large animal, much less anything so large with wings. The villagers brought grain, flowers, etc. from their homes and offered them to the flying elephant, who ate them all up. After eating so much, he went into the state of *nasha* [intoxication], and in that state of intoxication he first went out of his senses and then later fell asleep. Meanwhile, Lord Indra was anxiously wondering: 'Why has my elephant not come back after such a long time?'—and went out to search for him. Lord Indra saw the hardship which Arawat had caused the villagers, and heard their prayers asking that Arawat be removed from their village. Lord Indra became angry, cut off both of Arawat's wings, and gave one to the banana tree and the other to the peacock. Thus the elephant was deprived of his wings, and Lord Indra left him on earth for good. And from that time onwards the elephant has always remained on earth—and both the peacock and the banana tree were much enhanced: the one with great feathers, the other with large feather-leaves." [ID]

According to the artist:

"This is about the traits and behaviors of a tiger. A tiger retires to its cave at sunrise and sleeps the whole day, and in the evening at sunset it awakens with a loud roar, thumping the ground with its tail. The leopard, hearing the roar of the tiger, gives out an alarm of its own. And a bird called the *tiltila* bird [the male sandpiper, not shown] echoes the sound through the jungle. The message of the tiger is clear to every animal in the jungle. The message is: 'I've given you an entire day to do whatever you want to do, but, from this point on, any animal

Fig. 18.
Tiger[111]
2006
By Venkat Raman Singh Shyam (1970-)
Acrylic on canvas
39¼ x 69½"

that comes my way—be it an insect like the scorpion, or a bird like the peacock, or a deer—is food for me.' Then the animals, knowing the direction from which the tiger's roar has come, try to stay away from its path. This is what this picture depicts. It sleeps at sunrise, awakens at sunset and hunts at night—and thus the sun and moon are depicted. I experienced this myself at Ranthambore [a national park and tiger sanctuary], where I'd gone to do an exhibition."

[VRSS & JHB]

Fig. 19.
Death and the Woodpecker[112]
2002
by Venkat Raman Singh Shyam (1970-)
Acrylic on canvas
45¾ x 30¼"

According to the artist:

"Yamadev [God of Death] or his *doots* [messengers] used to come and take man to heaven when his time on earth was completed. One day the time for the woodpecker's death came, and Yamadev sent his *doots* to bring him to heaven. The woodpecker was a very good architect and sculptor, and famous for his craftsmanship. He had built for himself a seven-storied palace in the *semal* tree[113] [the leaves of which are depicted at the top of this painting]. When a *doot* came to the woodpecker and informed him to come with them to heaven, the woodpecker became very sad and then thought of some way to evade death. He asked the *doot*: 'Sir, I want to offer you at least a glass of water inside my palace, to show my gratitude. Then I will accompany you to wherever you wish.' The *doot* followed him to the top floor of the palace, where the woodpecker cleverly imprisoned him in a room which exactly fitted his form.

"When the first *doot* failed to return, Yamadev sent another. The woodpecker also locked him in the next floor below the first. In this way the woodpecker imprisoned all Yamadev's seven *doot*s in his palace. Finally, Yamadev himself came to earth in search of his missing messengers [his eyes are shown here, amidst the leafy branches]. He went to the woodpecker and asked for their whereabouts, but the woodpecker professed ignorance; so Yamadev continued to search many other places—to no avail. Then one day, sitting below a *mahua* tree,[114] the god saw many birds drinking the nectar of the *mahua*'s flowers, and thereafter becoming intoxicated and merry. He decided to use *mahua* liquor as a means for extracting the truth from those he wished to question. He transformed himself into a human and prepared a brew using *mahua* flowers. Among the many to whom he gave this brew were an ironsmith and the woodpecker. After getting drunk, they began to argue with each other, boasting about their individual skills, and the woodpecker bragged that the craftsmanship of his palace so impressed Death's *doot*s that he could overwhelm and imprison them therein.

"Yamadev heard all this and then released his *doot*s from their prison. After that he decided that no earthling will be given advance warning of his death, which would come suddenly to all. Also, no one would be allowed to come to heaven with his body—only their souls could enter heaven. So after that day, Yamadev disappeared from earth.

"In this painting, I have shown Yamadev, his seven messengers, and the woodpecker—who I've shown in the style of Swaminathan-ji's crow."[115] [ID]

Fig. 20.
Dharti Dai
2006
by Venkat Raman Singh Shyam (1970-)
Ink on paper
20 x 12"

According to the artist:

"Long, long ago, Bara Dev—Shiva—created the earth from balls of clay gathered from beneath the ocean [as explained in the *Creation of the Earth* myth, Figs. 6-9]. At that time Jalharin Matta [the Insect Mother who lives in the ocean and waters] and Bara Deo gave grace to Dharti Matta [Mother Earth] so that she could support plants, animals, humans and other creatures. Jalharin Matta and Bara Deo provided Shesh Nag [Lord Vishnu's great snake] as Dharti Matta's means of support on the waters. Bara Dev also gave light to Dharti Matta, in the form of Chandra Dev [the Moon God]. Jalharin Matta and Bara Deo ordered Dharti Matta to give the newly created Gonds all the water, air, food and necessary means for their subsistence. Dharti Matta agreed, and since then she has provided the Gonds with many blessings. Here she is shown with the moon behind her head, while holding her hands in benediction. Beneath her hands appear flowers symbolizing food. The hills of the earth (including the Vindhyachal and Satpura mountain ranges) are signified by the zig-zag patterns on her dress. Although Bara Deo and Jalharin Matta ordered Dharti Matta to be benevolent, I feel that these days humanity makes so many *atyaachar* [transgressions] against her that she must be sad, and that's how I've here shown the expression on her face." [ID]

Fig. 21.
Ganesh Kekra
2003
by Venkat Raman Singh Shyam (1970-)
Ink on paper with watercolour tinting
25 x 19$^7/_8$"

According to the artist:

"Several thousand years ago, in the times of the gods and goddesses, Lord Shiva and Parvati [his consort] were living in the Himalayas on Mount Kailash. Parvati became estranged from him and moved from Kailash to the forest. Living there alone, she felt the need for protection, so she removed some earth from her body, gave it the shape of a child, and put life into the form and thus created Ganesh. She said to him 'Son, I am going to the spring to take a bath, and while I'm there you should not allow anyone to approach me.' About that very time, Lord Shiva proceeded to meet Parvati Mata [Mother Parvati]. When he reached the spot where Parvati was living, he found Ganesh standing as the security guard at the gate. Lord Shiva did not ask anything from the security guard, but continued to proceed ahead. Then Ganesh stopped him, saying that he would not allow him to go any further; but Lord Shiva did not listen to him, and quarreled with Ganesh. In anger, god Shiva severed the head of Ganesh with his *trishul* [trident]—and where it fell no one knew. When Shiva reached Parvati he was elated to see her. Parvati asked Lord Shiva the whereabouts of his son, whom he must have met along the way. Then Shiva asked her: 'Which son are you talking about?' And Parvati told Lord Shiva: 'Since you were not here to guard me, I created Ganesh from the dirt of my body, and he is very close and dear to me.' Lord Shiva felt very worried, and told her that he had already killed Ganesh. Parvati said: 'Wherever you have killed him, take me there.' Both of them went to that place and found Ganesh's torso, they could not find his head. In anger Parvati started crying and told Lord Shiva: 'If you don't bring my son back to life, then I shall feel very bad about it!' But Lord Shiva replied: 'Ganesh is now dead, how can I bring him back to life?' Yet Parvati insisted. So Lord Shiva began to instill life into the child's torso, but said the head would have come from another living being—and thus would not resemble the original head. Shiva told his messengers to go in search of a living being lying asleep behind its mother. After a very long and thorough search, the messengers found a she-elephant sleeping with her back turned towards her children, who were also asleep. The messengers severed the head of one of her children, and brought it to Lord Shiva, who then fit it onto Ganesh's torso.

"When the she-elephant woke up and was surprised to find the head of one of her children missing, she started crying. While she was in this condition, her companions narrated to her what had happened. She then went, weeping, to ask Lord Shiva to return her child's head, saying: 'For the sake of your own child you severed the head of mine—what will now happen to my child? If a god can do this, other living beings can do anything!' Shiva then gave her a boon, and said: 'Although this dead body cannot be revived in the same form, yet it will be reborn without a head, which will be inside its torso—with the eyes attached to the torso itself. It will have a new name—*kekra* [crab]—and would not be known as her son. This is how the birth of Ganesh and the *kekra* took place. In this picture I have shown Ganesh three times: as created out of the dirt of Parvati's body, as Shiva's son, and how his origin led to the creation of the crab." [ID]

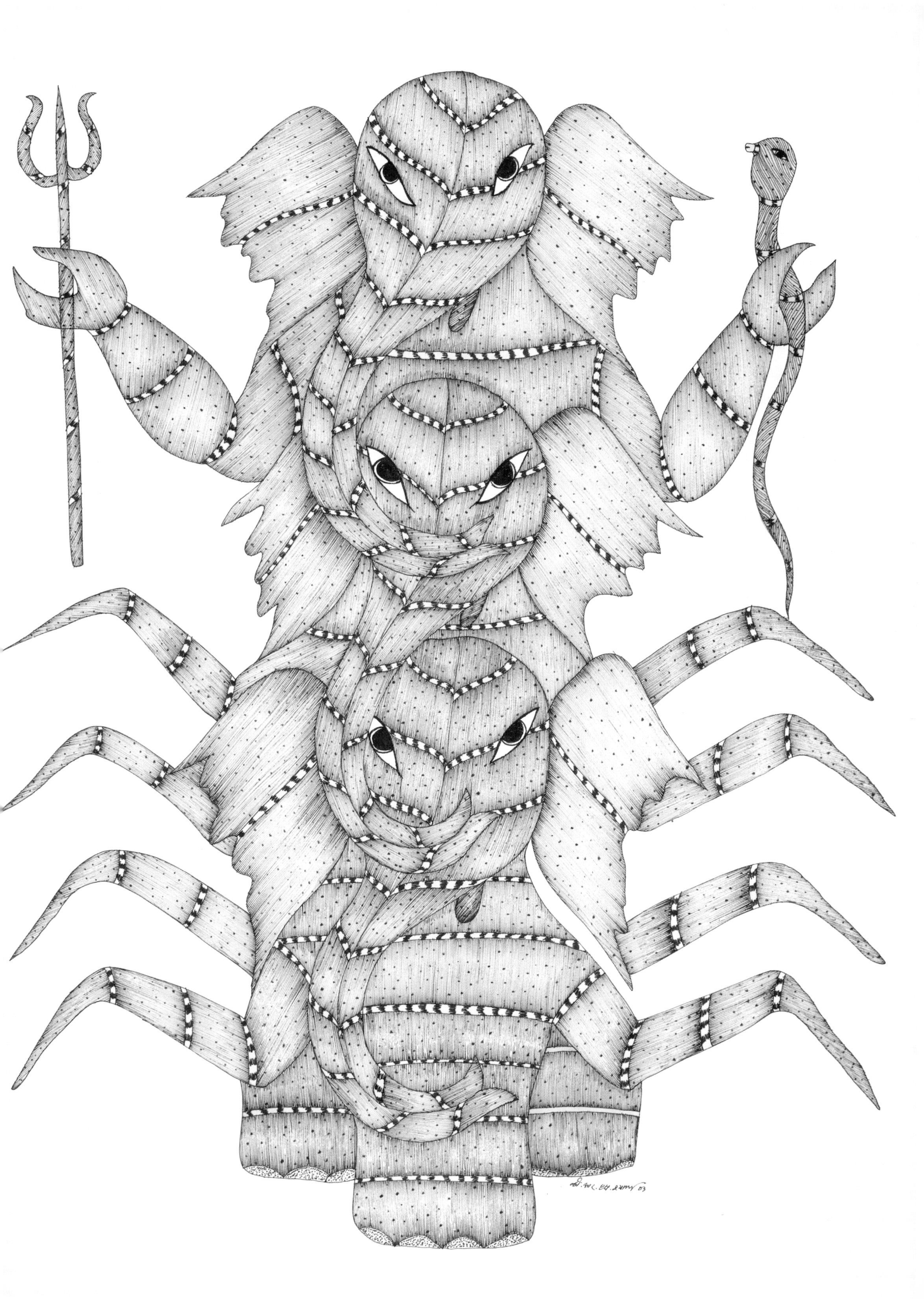

Fig. 22.
The Adivasis Learn How to Dance Like a Peacock
2005
by Rajendra Shyam
(1974-)
Acrylic on canvas
34½ x 22"

According to the artist:

"The peacock sees the dark clouds during the monsoon, and gets overjoyed, and in that state it spreads its feathers and dances with great abandon. At that time mankind worships the gods, plants their fields with seeds, and sings gaily while playing the *chatkora* [small wooden cymbals], the *maadar* [a hollow terracotta vessel, with two leather coverings at each open-mouthed side] and the *timki* [small upright terracotta drum]. The tribal men and women's feet and legs are unsteady when they start dancing, and they wonder how they'll be able to dance. Then they remember the peacock, and feel inspired to dance like the peacock.

"In this painting the tribals come out from their homes singing the Karma song: "*Dadar upper gouwn sai, nau kuri chani, manjur jhali jahaneel bagar hai, Raiiii...* ['The village is settled above a mound/hillock, innumerable peacock feathers are shown as the blue sky...']" And they sing other, similar songs. The *adivasis* [tribals] dress themselves just like the peacock; they wear *paijaniya* [jangling anklets], *chhalbal* [wristbands made of silver], *bohata* [silver armlets], *mohar* and *sutya* [necklaces]—and on their head they tie the feathers of the peacock in the form of a *kalgi* [the peacock's feather crest].

"Seeing these tribals dancing, the peacock also becomes quite happy, and then spreads its wings and sheds its feathers, which are then offered to the Thakur Dev [the village deity], and thereafter collected by the *ojha* [a healing priest and diviner] who waves them above sick persons to cure disease. Before the crop is sown, the grains are offered on leaf plates to Thakur Dev." [ID]

Fig. 23.
The Bana as Bara Deo
2006
by Rajendra Shyam
(1974-)
Acrylic and ink on paper
13⁵/₈ x 9"

According to the artist:

"There was a husband and wife who had seven sons. They lived together and had a common crop which they jointly tended, harvested, winnowed and threshed. Then the eldest said that it would be better if each of them did a distinct task of his own. The eldest—the Gond—decided to be a farmer. Because the farmer would need implements, the second one—the Agaria—was assigned the work of the blacksmith. The third became the Bardhai, the carpenter; the fourth—the Kumhar—worked as a potter. The fifth—the Tamer—took up the work of the brass metalworker. The sixth—the Baiga—brought wood and timber from the forest necessary for making various agricultural tools. The seventh and youngest brother—the Pardhan—asked what work would be assigned to him. The eldest brother told him that he should be engaged in the worship of Bara Deo, and to go to the various houses and perform the *bana* [a three-stringed musical instrument played with a bow, as shown on page 18], sing the praises of Bara Deo and other gods, goddesses, Gond *rajas* and other heroes. But the Pardhan did not know how to play the *bana*, so he looked reverently at the sky and noticed the *bharhi* bird [the long-billed pipit[116]] flying up and down, beautifully singing and making swooping sounds with its flight. Then it occurred to him that he should imitate the flight of the *bharhi* birds with his bow on the strings of the *bana* while singing songs and narrating stories.

"The seven brothers thereafter lived in separate houses, and thus each required separate portions of the harvest. The eldest brother asked the youngest which portion of the threshing floor he would choose for the grain. And the youngest, thinking that the maximum amount would come from the centre, asked for that—not realizing that most of the grain would shift towards the periphery. Accordingly he got very little—only one *soopa* [a winnowing basket] of grain. His livelihood has ever since been based on singing and reciting stories.

"The youngest brother went to the forest and noticed how the breezes blowing through a bowed branch of the *saja* tree[117] made a beautiful sound. So he thought, why not establish the worship of Bara Deo in the shade of the *saja* tree, and that is how the worship of Bara Deo, the principal deity of the Gond, started. The Pardhan is also known as *Pathari* [one who narrates religious stories] or *Dasondhi* [one who visits ten villages]. 'Par-dhan' means one who lives on the grain produced by others [*dhan* is the word for grain, *par* meaning 'on']. When the Pardhan would visit a farmer, then the news would go around throughout the village that the Pardhan had come, and in the evening people would gather to hear stories and songs all night long until sunrise, and in the morning the Pardhan would offer prayers to the gods and goddesses; and after the house had been cleaned and purified then he would ask for *dan* [an offering] and donations—which could include portions of the harvest, clothing, jewelry, money, food, livestock and other possessions.

"This picture shows our supreme deity, Bara Deo, in the form of the *bana*. Two *bharhi* birds appear flying out from behind the *bana*, three snakes here appear as tuning pegs, and one other represents the undulating bow. The snake is worshipped as both an ancestor and a representative of Lakshmi and Dharti Matta [the Goddess of Wealth and Mother Earth], and as a sacred being in its own right. The leather surface of the *bana* is made of the intestine of the cow or buffalo. Mare's hair is used as the strings, and requires the application of resin to tauten the strings. I've shown the face of the Bara Dev here as peaceful and contemplative." [ID]

Fig. 24.
Tithi Pakshi
2006
by Rajendra Shyam
(1974-)
Acrylic and ink on canvas
35 x 23¼"

According to the artist:

"When Bhagawan [God] created this universe in seven days, in the first three and a half days he created Prithvi [Earth] and all the living creatures. It took another full three and a half days for him to make the peacock; this was because the peacock is so beautiful and has such intricate designs. When Bhagawan was fitting all the parts of the peacock together, he left its feet for the last. Just as he was about to attach the feet onto the peacock's body, the *tithi* bird arrived. It thought: 'The peacock is already such a beautiful bird, why shouldn't I take its feet into my own body?' This angered Bhagawan, who cursed the *tithi* bird—that it should always live in fear of the sun in the day, and of other things at night and all other times—and would never be able to live peacefully; and thus when the *tithi* bird lays eggs she would have to guard them all day and night.

"The *tithi* bird lays eggs in the month of *Baisakh* [April-May, just before the rains arrive]. Thereafter she sits on her eggs throughout the hot summer for fear that a branch of the tree—or even a cloud—might fall on them. At night she lies on her back, on top of her eggs—with her feet and legs pointing upwards, to protect her eggs in case the sky falls down. Thus the *tithi* bird imagines.

"This picture shows both the male and female *tithi* birds protecting their eggs. The female and male birds look alike and behave the same. Both of them sit on the eggs together. When the chicks of this bird are hunted by the villagers, they can be caught by bare hands; but the adults are too fast and cannot be caught. During my childhood I've also caught these birds. I would feed them with grain, and then after some time let them free. I have never eaten them; perhaps others have. It can be great fun to chase and catch the chicks. Here I have shown the *tithi*s with their beaks open, as these birds are always making noises so as to scare away any predator or threat. Above the *tithi* bird is a cloud in the form of a tree. I haven't yet done a similar painting showing just the cloud in its own form. I sketched out the whole composition and filled in the lower, coloured areas; my wife—following my sketch—filled in the form of the tree. Just below the eggs I've shown the grass and small pebbles on which the eggs are laid. The yellow dots are the small pebbles, which are formed into a circular nest." [ID]

It is noteworthy to observe how this traditional Gond description of the *tithi* bird—so reminiscent of the paranoid "Chicken Little" in Western folklore—also closely reflects its actual behavior. The *tithi* (also known as the *titeeri* or "redwattled lapwing") has been ornithologically characterized as "uncannily and ceaselessly vigilant, day or night, and foremost to detect intrusion and raise the alarm."[118] [JHB]

Fig. 25. (below)
Seven Sisters
2000
by Subhash Vyam
(1970-)
Wood sculpture,
26½ x 11½ x 9"

This sculpture depicts a favorite Pardhan Gond story—about an impoverished elderly couple "cursed" with the burden of seven daughters to support. With so many mouths to feed they often must go hungry. Out of desperation, the father abandons the girls one day in the jungle, and the remainder of the story (which is usually long and rambling) tells of their various ordeals; according to what version of the story is being told, the girls may or may not be happily reunited with their parents at the end. Subhash and his wife Durga Bai's joint telling of the tale is especially long, and must be published elsewhere. Instead, the artist Rajendra Singh Shyam's version is here presented (see text accompanying Fig.26, below).

Subash has chosen to depict an early passage in the story—in which the family's desperation and hunger are vividly described. Carved using simple tools, from a single block of wood, this sculpture powerfully captures the trauma of poverty and hunger, such as the sculptor and his own family had experienced in the past (see page 32). [JHB]

Fig. 26. (right)
Seven Sisters
2004
by Rajendra Shyam (1974-)
Acrylic on canvas
34¾ x 24½"

According to the artist:

"There was an old woodcutter and his wife who had seven daughters. Woodcutters' earnings are meager—and far from sufficient to feed so many mouths. One day he was tempted to eat *kheer* (a pudding prepared with milk, rice and sugar), and asked his wife to make it at night when the girls were already asleep, so that it need not be shared. But the wife had only half-cooked the *kheer* when, one by one, all the girls woke up—and then obviously the small bowl of pudding had to be shared between nine people.

"The old man then decided to take all the girls into the jungle the next day and leave them to their destiny there. The next morning he asked the youngest girl to look for lice in his hair. When the girl removed the turban from her father's head she found small berries of the *chaar* tree[119] tucked within it, and then all the girls wanted more berries. The man immediately agreed to take them to the jungle where they could collect as many *chaar* berries as they desired. The unsuspecting girls happily accompanied him deep into the jungle. Once there the father left them near a *chaar,* saying he would be cutting wood nearby. The old man hung his axe and the empty *tumba* [a dried gourd with a hole used for carrying and serving water] from

the top of a tree near the tree where the girls were picking berries, and then left for home bearing a load of wood. [The *tumba* and axe are here depicted hanging in the centre of the tree.]

"By evening the girls were thirsty and called out to their father. Their voices echoed from the empty dried gourd bottle, which repeatedly tapped against the axe with a thud, so that the girls thought their father was still nearby at work and thus stopped worrying. However, they grew thirstier and, after searching for him in vain, the youngest climbed to the top of the *semal* tree[120] and from there spotted a pool in a clearing outside the jungle. She climbed down and they all headed for the pool. But as they approached the pool its water disappeared. The girls realized that the deity of the pool wanted an offering. The youngest one had *mundari* [a ring] on her finger, and the eldest threw it into the centre of the pool. The pool again brimmed with crystal cool water, with which the girls quenched their thirst. The girls decided to return home on their own when the youngest suddenly remembered her ring and wanted it back from her eldest sister. The sister tried to pacify her but to no avail. Finally, the eldest went into the pond in search of the ring and kept singing: 'The water is up to my ankle, and I can't find your ring; the water is up to my knee, and I can't find your ring; the water is up to my waist and I can't find your ring; the water is up to my shoulder, and I can't find your ring...' and then she reached the centre of the pool and sang: '...the water is up to my head and here I have found your ring!' and then she threw the ring to her sister.

"Meanwhile, the other sisters had left as it was getting late and only the youngest one remained waiting for their eldest sister to return. But she did not return. The youngest sister climbed on to a nearby tree and waited and waited, crying all the time. A king and his company, while returning from their hunting, sat under the tree—and one of the youngest sister's tears dropped onto the king's lap. He asked his men to taste it, to find out what it was; it was a clear night so it couldn't possibly be rain. They tasted the drop and confirmed that it was a human tear. A light was lit and they searched the tree in vain, but then a man with just one eye spotted the girl sitting on its highest branch. Although the king ordered the girl to be brought down, nobody was able to climb the tree to fetch her. Finally a man who limped climbed the tree and brought the girl down.

"The youngest girl was very beautiful and the king took her to his palace and married her. The king already had six wives, but none had borne him a child. The girl became his seventh wife, and in a few days she was pregnant. The rest of the queens were jealous and, as soon as the child was born, they threw him on the *ghura* [garbage pile] and told the king that the youngest queen gave birth to a *lodha* [stone mortar]. The king was furious and deported the girl to the fields, where she was given the job of *kaua hakauni* [one who chases away the crow]. The child however grew as fast as the garbage pile grew. The queens were worried and threw him into the *saar* [cowshed]. The child was fed milk by the cows there, and grew even faster. The queens then put the child into the *ghoda-saar* [horse corral], but thereafter found him merrily enjoying a horse ride. Finally, they threw him into the same pool where the eldest sister disappeared. In a few days' time the king's hunting party again rested under the same tree on the bank of the pool, upon which they spotted two beautiful alluring flowers. All the hunting party—including the king—tried to catch one of the flowers, but it could not be reached. Everyone else was called to try, including the six queens, but all of them failed. At last somebody remembered the youngest queen, and she was sent for with a carriage and the gift of new clothes and jewelry. As she climbed down from the carriage and into the waters, the flower came on its own into her lap and turned into a lovely child. Likewise, the other flower also came and, as soon as she plucked it, it turned into her eldest sister. The girl and the king were overjoyed. The king also married the eldest sister, banished the previous six wives from his palace, and they all lived happily ever after." [SS]

Fig. 27.

Doors Decorated with Birds and Surrounded by Dignas

1997

by Durga Bai Vyam

(1974-)

Blue poster paint and orange poster paint into which *lal mitti* (red clay) has been mixed—painted on paper

9¾ x 12"

According to the artist:

"This picture shows a house door made of wood, the outside of which has been embellished with relief carvings of birds. Surrounding it are moulded and mud-coloured *dignas* [auspicious zig-zag decorative motifs]." [ID]

The Gonds traditionally apply carved and/or painted designs to embellish doors and surrounding areas. At right is a photograph of Durga Bai at the home of her in-laws in the village of Sonpuri (next to Patangarh, Madhya Pradesh). The doors and surrounding *digna* design were painted by Ganga Ram Vyam. [JHB]

Fig. 28.
The Story of a Parrot and a Woman
2007
by Durga Bai Vyam
(1974-)
Acrylic on canvas
43¾ x 34⅜"

According to the artist:

"I have painted the *salhe* tree[121] in the form of the Earth Mother. The tree is populated with people and birds—such as the *pareva* [pigeons]—who live on its branches, and animals such as monkeys, rats, deer.

"Inside a big hole in the tree resides a parrot in his nest. Charmed by the parrot's sweet words and melodious voice, a woman begins to bring him delicious treats such as *kheer* [a milk, rice and sugar pudding], *puris* [fried wheat cake] and other delights. This devotion to the parrot makes the woman's husband extremely jealous. He seeks the parrot out from the hole in the tree and makes him fly away, while he himself climbs into the hole.

"When the woman comes the next day with food for the parrot, the husband mimics the parrot's sweet words and tricks his wife into leaving the sumptuous food she has cooked for the parrot. The following day, however, the wife discovers the husband's ploy and becomes angry. The husband tries to appease her and pledges to find the parrot and bring him back. When he finally returns with the parrot, a big iron cage is built for the parrot and he is fed delicious food again. The parrot begins to play host for all those who come to visit the home of the man and wife, charming them with his sweet words.

"From that day on, men and women domesticated the parrot, which came to be considered a symbol of good luck, health and prosperity. In the month of *Saawan* [July/August], when the rains come pouring down, Gonds feed *kheer* and *puris* to parrots, mynas and other birds. [In this picture] the houses in the village hills are depicted, with people communing with birds and looking after them." [RV]

Fig. 29.
Shri Badhawan Dev and Badhawan Devi (The God and Goddess of Increased Grain)
1999
by Durga Bai Vyam
(1974-)
Gouache on paper
19½ x 24¼"

According to the artist:

"Badhawan Dev and Badhawan Devi increase the quantity of food. After the farmer reaps the harvest and brings it to the threshing floor, he starts winnowing it and then collects the grain, offers it to Shri Badawan Dev and Devi and does *puja* [worship]. This annual *puja* includes his sacrificing a boar—that's a pig—and a cock. This makes the god happy and he increases the production or quantity of the grain. Then the next day the people put the grain into a *kaavar* [a double-sided carrying yoke, shown left of centre] and the *gon* [a bag]—here shown being stitched up in preparation for filling it with paddy and loading onto a buffalo to transport home, where it will be kept in the *lilali kothi* [storehouse].

"A woman [bending down, at centre] sweeps the threshing floor before the paddy is placed on it. The ground is soaked with water so that it will settle down, and then *gobar* [cow dung] is spread on the floor; only then is it swept. Before any work begins a *puja* is done—including offerings of a coconut, the paddy basket and a bottle of liquor [all shown at top centre].

"A woman at upper left is carrying rice on her head, and uses a staff to help steady her balance. She takes the bullocks home after their day's work is completed. All three bullocks shown [near left margin] are loaded with rice, and a dog trails behind the woman.

"There is a pole in the centre of the threshing floor, and attached to it one sees a cord with loops for tying around the necks of the bullocks—who walk around the pole, on top of the rice-paddy stock, so as to pound the grain and thereby separate it from the chaff [the rice and chaff are shown here as the yellow, white and red striped area, right of centre and under the tether]. Below the rice and chaff is shown a sleeping watchman, who guards the rice all night against theft, fire, and both domestic and wild animals. This watchman is always a member of the family; his axe is shown beneath him. In the lower right corner someone is winnowing the rice in a *soopa* [winnowing basket]. The sacrificial pig, cock and hen appear tethered to a short stake [bottom centre of the picture], and Shri Badhawan Dev and Badhawan Devi appear in the upper right corner." [ID]

The painting below shows a rare, early example of Durga Bai Vyam's formative style. Its subject matter is also depicted and described by the artist in the upper right corner of Fig. 29. [JHB]

According to the artist:

"This is an older work of mine. I was experimenting at this stage with the *nag muri* [a pattern Durga Bai developed, inspired by the *nag muri*, a serpent-like silver armlet, often worn by her grandmother] and the *dandiwala* [horizontal lined] patterns. I primed this whole cloth with *churri mitti* [white clay], on top of which I applied *kala mitti* [black clay]—as well as some highlighting with poster paints. Shri Badhawan Dev ensures a bountiful crop. The grain is shown here in the centre [as a vertically striped oval form]." [ID]

Fig. 30.
***Shri Badhawan Dev (The God of Increased Grain)**, 1997*
by Durga Bai Vyam
Clay pigments and poster paints on canvas
26 x 20½"

Fig. 31. (below)
Baasin Kunya is Shot by her Youngest Brother[122]
2004
by Durga Bai Vyam
(1974-)
Acrylic on canvas
30¼ x 20½"

Fig. 32. (right page)
The Creation of Bamboo
2004
by Durga Bai Vyam
Acrylic on canvas
31¾ x 21"

Here follows the artist Durga Bai's telling of the myth of Bassin Kunya [the Bamboo Maiden]—which she learned from her *dadi* [paternal grandmother]:

"This is the story of the birth of Baasin Kunya. In one home there lived seven brothers and one sister, whose name was Sundaria. The seven brothers farmed and Sundaria used to look after the household work—cleaning, cooking, washing, etc. One day, while chopping wet leafy vegetables, she suddenly cut her finger, and blood started flowing profusely. She had no piece of cloth with which to wipe the blood, so she used a leafy vegetable itself to wipe the blood. When in the evening the brothers came home for dinner, she served them a dish called *bhajji* [fried greens]—comprised of that blood-smeared leafy vegetable. They asked her again and again: 'Today the *bhajji* is very, very delicious; what is it that you've added to make it so delicious?' until she felt compelled to tell them that her finger got cut, and there was no piece of cloth nearby on which to wipe the blood, so she used the leafy vegetable itself. Six of her brothers thought: 'If the vegetable with her blood had become so delicious, imagine how delicious her meat would be!' Thinking thus, the six brothers planned to kill her.

"But the seventh brother refused to take part in the plan, as he loved his sister very much. One day, the six older brothers cajoled Sundaria into accompanying them into the jungle, where they made her climb a *simal* tree.[123] And then all the six brothers tried to shoot her with their bows and arrows, but none of them succeeded. The seventh brother was forced to shoot too. Although he closed his eyes and did not aim at her, nonetheless his arrow hit her and she died.

"The six brothers told the seventh brother: 'Go to the forest, gather six pieces of dry firewood and, without tying them, bring them here.' The seventh brother went into the forest and there he met the seven sisters of a snake, and he told them what had happened. They then told him to collect the seven pieces of wood, which they would bind for him [by winding their bodies around the wood]. Then his brothers asked him to bring water in a pitcher perforated by six holes; and he asked: 'How can I bring water in a pitcher with six holes, how will I bring it?' The frogs heard his problem and came to his rescue—by plugging up the holes from inside the pitcher. After he brought the water and roasted the meat of the sister, he was told to wash a piece of cloth without using a stone.[124] He again went to the river and started to cry. A tortoise and *bagula* bird [heron] heard his cries and said: 'We'll help you.' The *bagula* touched the cloth and made it white, and the tortoise offered his shell to serve as a beating stone.

"Then the seventh brother thought: 'If I go home then I will be asked to eat the meat of my sister.' Again he started crying.

Then the fish and the crab came to his aid. They said: 'Kill us, and when they tell you to eat meat eat the fish instead, and when they tell you to eat the bone, then eat the crab. In this manner you should save yourself from eating the flesh of your sister.' So when he went home and was served her meat, he hid it behind his back and instead ate the meat of the fish and the bone of the crab. At night, after all his other brothers fell asleep, he took his sister's meat and buried it in the back yard, and watered that place. After a few days a green and very luxuriant bamboo began to grow.

"One day a cowherd—who was taking his cattle for grazing—passed by and noticed a very green and nice growth of bamboo and he thought: 'Why not cut this tree? It will serve as fodder for the cattle.' Just as he started cutting the bamboo he heard a voice say: 'Cut me slowly. I nurture you, I nourish you.' He cut and took the bamboo and told everyone what he had heard. Eventually this news reached the seventh brother. He went there and he recollected what happened earlier, saying: 'This is my own sister, she was earlier Sundaria, now she is Baasin Kuniya [the Bamboo Maiden].' Since then, this Baasin Kuniya nurtures and nourishes everyone. Heeas [a caste of bamboo craftsmen] make flutes out of it, and use it and sing everywhere, and thereby earn their livelihood. No one's marriage is complete until the bamboo is ceremonially affixed in the ground to sanctify the *mandap* [place of marriage]. Bamboo has other ceremonial uses. When a child is born it is first placed on a bamboo winnowing fan and only then put on its mother's lap and allowed to start breast-feeding. To ensure a good harvest, a bamboo pole is placed in the centre of a field at the time of the Hareli festival [known in Hindi as the 'Hariyali' festival, it is held on the last day of the month of *Shravan* (July/August), in celebration of both the birth of Lakshmi (goddess of wealth), and the new growth of *hari* (green) following the monsoon rains]. When someone dies, the last rites are performed on bamboo biers. At the Diwali festival [another festival in honour of Lakshmi, held in October], the Aheers[125] worship Lakshmi by making bowers of bamboo." [ID]

This is one of Durga Bai's favorite myths, which she has often depicted in different manners and scales. These two examples excel in their balance of fine detail with bold colour and composition. [JHB]

In mainstream Hindu iconography, the deities Shiva and his consort Parvati are often shown accompanied by their respective mounts (the bull and the tiger or lion) and an entourage of devoted dwarf-like attendants, known in Sanskrit as *ganas*. While at first glance this seems to be what the artist Durga Bai has painted here, in fact these small figures represent the major Gond *gotras* (clans). Thus an apparently conventional Hindu image can include uniquely tribal significance. [JHB]

According to the artist:

"At the very time that Bara Dev [the 'Great God']—Shankar [Shiva]—is born on earth, then gradually by-and-by human beings are also born. Lord Shankar thought that once these human beings are born, then they will have children. And the children will grow and will become eligible for marriage. And when they become eligible for marriage, then where would they go? And how would their marriages take place? Which girl would get married to which

Fig. 33.
The Creation of the Clans
2001
by Durga Bai Vyam
(1974-)
Acrylic on canvas
23½ x 20"

boy? Thinking thus, Lord Shankar [here shown as the large mounted figure at left] determines the *gotra* [clan] of five such persons—you know *gotra*, everyone has a *gotra*, which means the ancestors from whom you've descended. And normally what happens is that, among those of the same *gotra*, marriages cannot take place. It has to take place with a person from another *gotra*. That is the thing. So here he [Shiva] has created the five *gotras*. The first—called Gangabansinetam—he let flow from his matted hair along the Ganga [River Ganges] and its streams. In the upper part of the matted hair of Lord Shankar was the moon, and there the *gotra* created was Chandramansigua. From his neck or the throat he created the third *gotra,* Nagbansi-Mahavir. The fourth was created from the lion, the mount of Parvati Mata [the Mother Goddess Parvati, Shiva's consort—here shown as the large mounted figure at right] and was called Singhbansi-Parteti. The fifth *gotra,* Sandia-Markan, was created by Lord Shankar from His mount Dudanadias. Thus Lord Shankar created the five *gotras* and sent them to live in their respective areas and rule there." [ID]

Fig. 34.
A Mother is Like a Tree
2007
by Suresh Singh Dhurvey
(1977-)
Ink on paper
12¼ x 9¼"

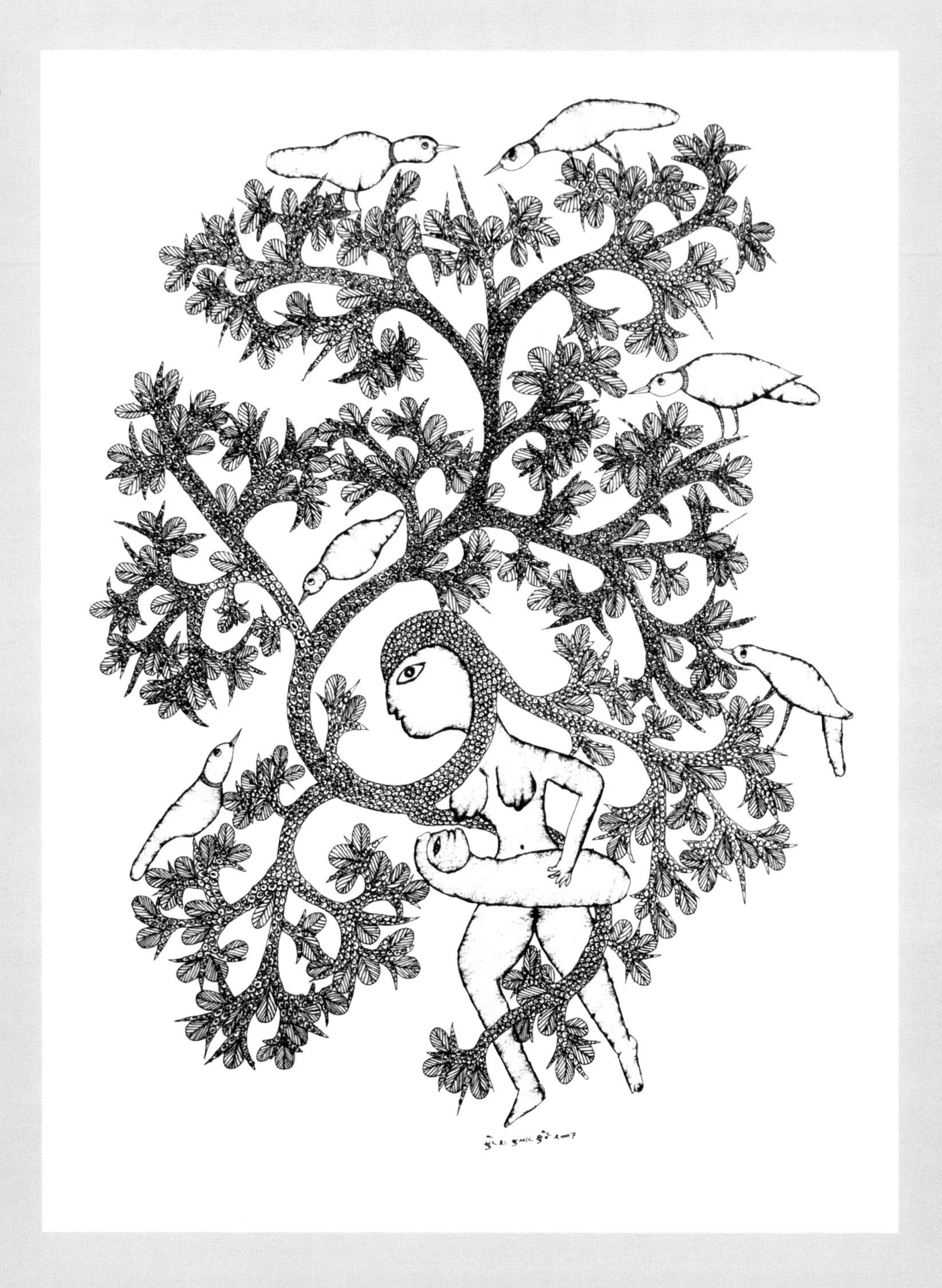

According to the artist:

"This is in the shape of my mother, and I've shown a tree growing out of her hair. Just as the tree provides shade, the mother provides shelter and nurturing to her child. Both the *bundi* and the *ghisni*[126] techniques have been used by me in this drawing. The *bundi* I now use is different from the simple dots I used when working with Jangarh. The *bundi* is here a dot enclosed in a circle." [ID]

According to the artist:

"This is the assistant of the Night Goddess Muhkuri. Together the two assume many forms and move about the village at night, helping people to find their ways or keeping lonely people company. At times only the sound of their voices can be heard—either singing or speaking. They fight the *tona toka* [evil charms]. On the whole Rat Mai Muhkuri is a benevolent deity whose place is made inside every household's kitchen. The place itself would be marked by a very small mud platform on which two or three small oven pots filled with grains [rice, *kodon* and *kutki*[127]] will be kept. She is specially worshipped on Dussera and Navakhai [the day when tribals in Madhya Pradesh and Chhattisgarh begin eating from the first fruits of the new harvest]." [SS]

Fig. 35.
Rat Mai Muhkuri's Assistant
2001
By Suresh Singh Dhurvey (1977-)
Ink on paper, 11 x 7"

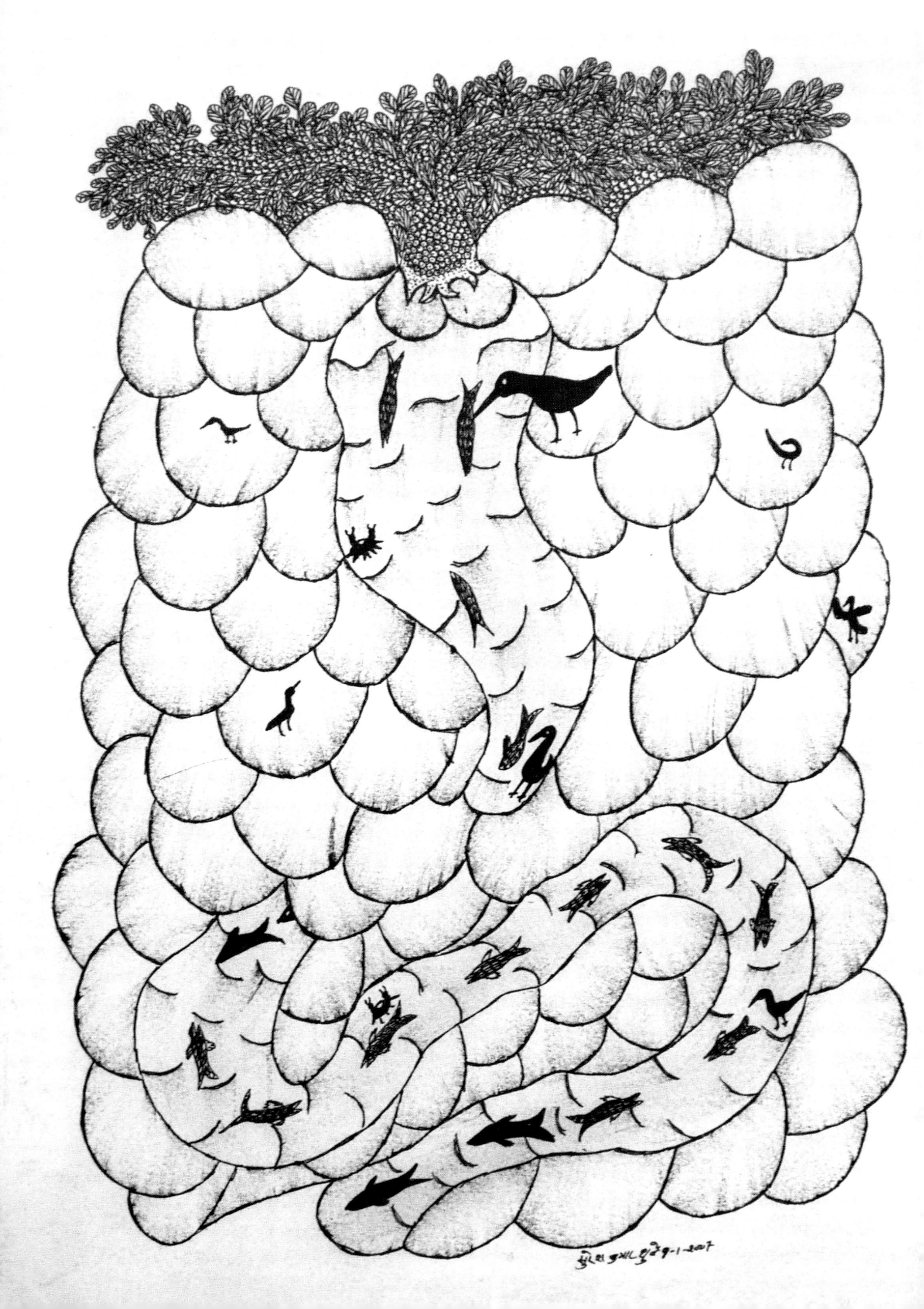

According to the artist:

"This depicts Narmada Mai [Our Mother Narmada River], whose source is in the mountains. As she came down, Bhim [a hero of legendary strength[128]] tried to stop her flow by stepping down upon her at Bhim Kundi [Bhim's Pool]. But Narmada continued on by, going underground for about a kilometer or so, and thereafter resurfaced, flowing easily. At the top of the picture I have shown the forest and mountains. In the river are fish and crabs, two *bagula* [heron] birds are catching fish [shown at centre], and there is also a *kilkila* [kingfisher] bird, which can dive underwater to catch fish [here shown on the rocks at centre left]. If you want to cross the Narmada here, it can be crossed thrice in that many jumps, because it's so narrow and meanders around so sharply. Before I did this drawing I coloured the paper with pink and blue powdered chalk—an idea that occurred to me while working with chalk at the Museum of Mankind."[129] [ID]

Fig. 36. (left page)
The Narmada at Bhim Kundi
2007
by Suresh Singh Dhurvey
(1977-)
Ink on yellow and blue chalk tinted paper
11¼ x 8 ¼"

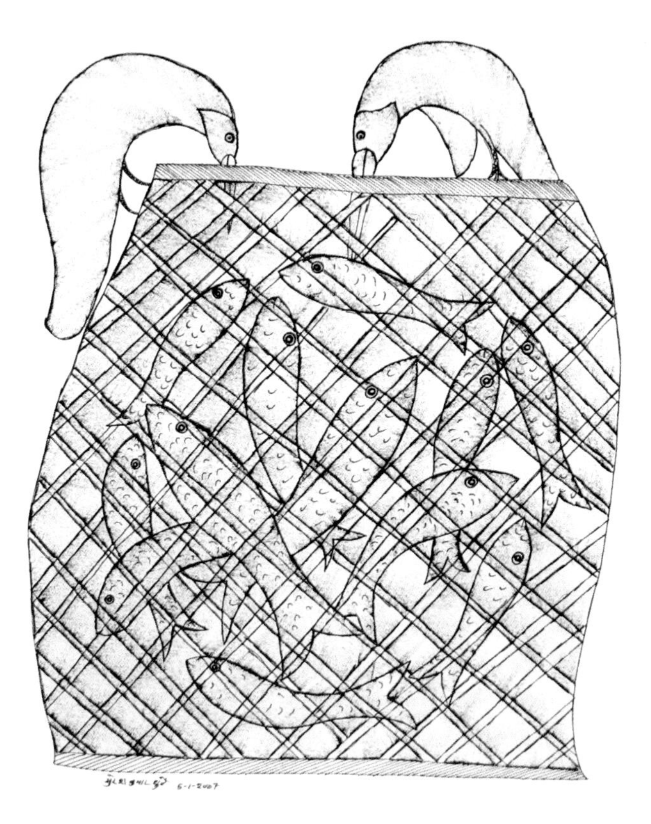

Fig. 37.
Kilkila Birds Eating Fish From a Basket
2007
by Suresh Singh Dhurvey
Ink on paper
8 x 10"

According to the artist:

"Here, I've just shown two *kilkila* [kingfishers] stealing fish from a fisherman's *tuti* [basket]." [ID]

Fig. 38.

Patangarh Talva, 2000
By Suresh Singh Dhurvey
(1977-)
Ink on paper, 12½ x 9"

According to the artist:

"The *talva* [tank] of Patangarh has a boundary of piled stones, some of which are very old and have carvings that originally belonged to the shrine of Thakur Dev—but are now piled up on its bank. In the middle of the tank can be seen a *khamb* [a wooden pillar or pole], represented here by a tree [shown at the top, centre]; it is said that this was the *khamb* which was dug as the central marriage pillar for the wedding of Jangarh's mother and father. This pole is now almost broken, but a part of it is still visible. At that time, the pond was still being dug, so it's not very old. The shape of the *talva* is long and zig-zags, and in parts fields project into it. Stones are shown piled along the right and left borders. Two curved areas [at the very top] are where people are shown bathing. Mud banks are in the middle, where a *kachayi* plant—called *beuj* in Hindi—is shown four times [in pot-like planters]. The juice of this plant's leaves is considered good for sore throat and runny nose, and tastes good too. Mud is often piled around these four plants. *Talvas* are used for bathing, washing, watering cattle and for fishing—but for only very small fish. Youngsters play in them too. Drinking water is not taken from the tank, but rather from the two wells. Children now climb on the *khamb* and from there jump into the water and play.

"This drawing was done in Bhopal, in recollection of happy memories. In very hot weather, half of the tank will dry up. One of the central parts of the tank [viz., the horizontal rectangle shown directly under the central circle] usually remains dry. The central circular area is a large round boulder used for washing clothes. People shown at upper right are taking water from the wells. The two represented trees are both *pipals*.[130] A smaller plant [just to the left of the top/central *pipal* tree] is a *beshram* [*Ipeomea*]." [SS]

Patangarh talva, 2006

Fig. 39.
Batua
2004
by Suresh Singh Dhurvey
(1977-)
Acrylic and ink on canvas
33½ x 20"

According to the artist:

"In earlier times, when there were no facilities for banks, people would put their silver coins in a *batua* [bag closed with strings] and bury it in the ground, often under a tree. And to mark the spot they would put a skull of an ox on the tree. Many times, when the owner of such hidden money dies, the *batua* place becomes *batua bhuta ah gaya* ['the money has turned haunted'], and whosoever tries to find it either dies or meets with some terrible mishap (like someone in the person's family falls ill, or gets bitten by a snake). There's a similar spot known in our village of Pathangarh—under a *pipal* [sacred fig[131]] tree—where many people have tried to find the buried treasure, to no avail. They finally cut down the tree and dug the whole place up, yet the money has not been found. Still, people continue to believe that treasure is there. Such treasure is supposed to be guarded by snakes, and that's why I have decorated the whole ground with snakes. Myna birds flank the tree." [SS]

Fig. 40.
Best of the Best, 2006
An episode from the animated film *The Tallest Tale Competition.* Directed and produced by Leslie MacKenzie. Script based on a traditional Gond story adapted by Peter Hynes. Music and hand-painted cels by Suresh Singh Dhurvey, Narmada Prasad, Ravi Prasad, Uday Pushyam, Shambhu Dhyaal Shyam, Anand Shyam, Dhanaya Shyam, Dilip Shyam, Kala Bai Shyam, Mayank Shyam, Mohan Shyam, Nankusia Shyam, Rajendra Shyam, Venkat Raman Singh Shyam, Gariba Tekam, Ravi Kumar Tekam and Durga Bai Vyam. Available in English, Gaelic, Hindi, Gondi, Marathi, Halbi, Santali and Saora.
Duration: 5 minutes, 6 seconds.

"Best of the Best" is a short, humourous, animated film inspired by a passage found within a longer, traditional Gond story.[132] The UK-based West Highland Animation company[133] produced this film in collaboration with an impromptu team of Pradhan Gond artists—who hand-painted the film's cels using their distinctive colour schemes and designs within a generic Gond style. It is the first animated film to present both an Indian tribal story and direct contributions from Indian tribal artists.

Another episode from the same animated films series, entitled "How the Elephant Lost His Wings", shows a mythic creature that recurs in ancient sources and different tribal traditions, and is depicted in this exhibition by Venkat Raman Singh Shyam's "The Flying Elephant" (Fig.17).[134] "How the Elephant Lost His Wings" was created by the Western artist/animator Tara Douglas, who based the episode's style on the Ghadwa caster tradition of Bastar.[135] Douglas subsequently co-founded the UK-based Adivasi Arts Trust[136], which has directly collaborated with tribal artists on other animation projects, through workshops co-sponsored by New Delhi's Indira Gandhi National Centre for the Arts, and other Indian institutions.

By combining foreign media, techniques and patronage with indigenous styles, artistry and narrative themes, such ventures converge the latest innovations of two reciprocally corresponding styles: Western "Primitivism" and contemporary "hybrid" tribal art. [JHB]

Leslie MacKenzie of West Highland Animation with the Pardhan Gond artist Kala Bai Shyam.

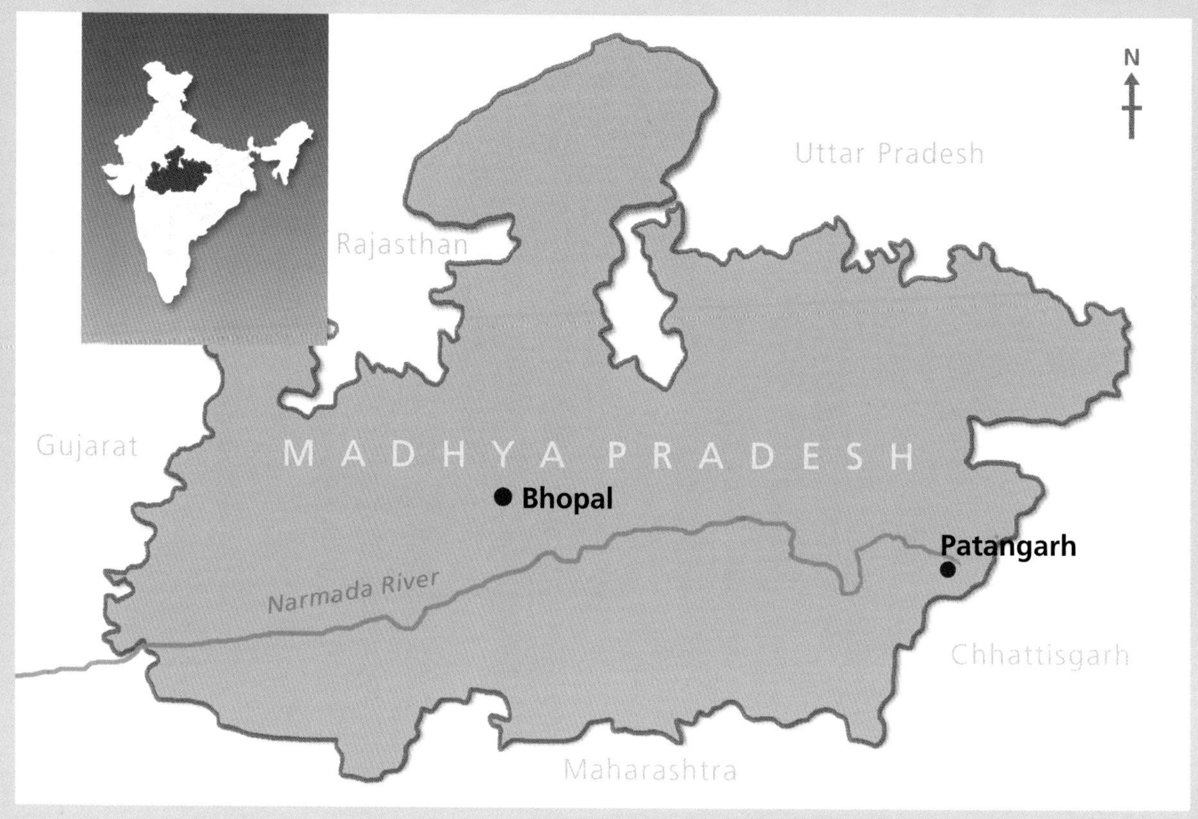

Distance between Bhopal and Patangarh: approx. 260 miles / 418 kilometers

ENDNOTES

[1] Quoted from a January 2007 interview translated by Hartosh Singh Bal. It warrants noting that Venkat is now learning English.

[2] "'Aesthetic' recognitions may be autonomous discoveries, but they are also forms of power [...] As we see increasingly with indigenous peoples around the world, traditionally the subject of anthropology's quest, the tropes available for the formulation of their identities are those formulated in the (distant) [sic] art world." George E. Marcus and Fred R. Myers, "The Traffic in Art and Culture: An Introduction", in *The Traffic in Culture, Refiguring Art and Anthropology*, eds. George E. Marcus and Fred R. Myers (Berkeley: University of California Press, 1995), p. 35.

[3] Relevant literature includes: Michael F. Brown, *Who Owns Native Culture?* (Cambridge, MA: Harvard University Press, 2003); Lynda Jessup, ed., *On Aboriginal Representation in the Gallery* (Quebec: Canadian Museum of Civilizations, 2002); Ivan Karp and Steven D. Lavine, eds., *Exhibiting Cultures, the Poetics and Politics of Museum Display* (Washington: Smithsonian Institution Press, 1991); Lucy R. Lippard, *Mixed Blessings, New Art in a Multicultural America* (New York: Pantheon Books, 1990); and Ruth B. Phillips and Christopher B. Steiner, eds. *Unpacking Culture: Art and Commodity in Colonial and Post Colonial Worlds* (Berkeley: University of California Press, 1999). Increasing curatorial involvement of tribal peoples can be found at a broad spectrum of institutions. In the US, for example, exhibitions curated by various American Indian authorities (including artists, tribal elders and academically credentialed scholars) can be found at modest community centers and museums at many American Indian reservations as well as at the National Museum of the American Indian in Washington, D.C.. Now, in India itself, an ethnographic museum called "Vacha: Museum of Voice" has been established by and for tribal communities, through an NGO named "Basha" (based in the town of Tejgarh—Tal. Chhota Udepur, Dist. Vadodara, Gujarat); for more information see: Vacha: Museum of Voice catalogue (Gujarat: Adivasi Academy; n.d.); and Ganesh N. Devy's *A Nomad Called Thief: Reflections on Adivasi Silence* (New Delhi: Orient Longman Pvt. Ltd., 2006), pp. 172-183. For a contrasting, illuminating account of non-indigenous approaches

to exhibiting tribal arts, see Sally Price's *Paris Primitive: Jacques Chirac's Museum on the Quai Branly* (Chicago: University of Chicago Press, 2007).

[4] Joseph Alsop, *The Rare Art Traditions: the History of Art Collecting and Its Linked Phenomena* (New York: Princeton University Press and Harper & Row, 1982), p. 127.

[5] Jyotindra Jain as quoted in John H. Bowles, "Arts and Crafts: An Interview with Jyotindra Jain", *The India Magazine of Her People and Culture*, August 1998, p. 34.

[6] It might be noted that Jangarh Singh Shyam was and is usually referred to—by both those in his tribal community and the outside art world—simply as "Jangarh" (sometimes transliterated as "Jangadh"). In keeping with the egalitarian and informal regard towards self and others prevalent among the Gonds, this essay will refer to Jangarh and other Gond artists initially by their full names, and thereafter by their first names.

[7] Kavita Singh, "Jangarh Singh Shyam and the Great Machine", *Marg* 53, no. 2 (December 2001): p.61.

[8] Epic droughts and famines between 1876-79 and 1896-1902 resulted in a shocking number of deaths throughout northern and central India—including the Narmada River valley, which at one point was described by American missionaries as "the great graveyard of India"(famine mortality estimates for central and northern India range between 12.2-29.3 million). See Mike Davis, *Late Victorian Holocausts, El Niño Famines and the Making of the Third World* (London and New York: Verso, 2001), pp. 7 and 154-5; Davis's book provides invaluable information and analysis of this much-ignored dark chapter of India's British colonial era.

[9] The break-up of the Pardhan Gond's patronage relationship with other Gond clans can be traced back to the early half of the 19th century; see Shamrao Hivale's *The Pardhans of the Upper Narbada Valley* (London: Oxford University Press, 1946), p.16. For further information about disruptive 19th century historical events affecting the Pardhan Gond communities described in this essay see R.R. Rudman's *Central Provinces District Gazetteers: Mandla District, Volume A, Descriptive* (Bombay: The Times Press, 1912), pp. 36-40. Regarding subsequent disruptions by Thugs active in and around the upper Narmada River valley, and general descriptions of the region's overall weak law-and-order conditions during the 19th century, see Mike Dash, *Thug: The True Story of India's Murderous Cult* (London: Granta Books, 2005).

[10] This quote from an anonymous informant appears in Hivale, *The Pardhans*, p. 16.

[11] Kalyan Kumar Chakravarty, "Tribal Identity: Extinction or Adaptation of the Gonds", in *Tribal Identity in India*, ed. Kalyan Kumar Chakravarty (Bhopal: Indira Gandhi Rashtriya Manav Sangrahalaya, 1996), pp. 284-5. To this day exotic stereotypes and racial prejudice—as well as conflicts over ethnic and cultural identity and different political interests—inevitably complicate any serious consideration of "tribal" cultures throughout India and elsewhere. Consideration of these sensitive issues goes well beyond the limits of this essay, wherein the Hindi word "adivasi" (meaning "original dwellers" or "indigenous people") is used interchangeably with "tribe" or "tribal", which in turn are used in the provisional way proposed by the Indian anthropologist Shyama Charan Dube in his *Tribal Heritage of India, Vol. I: Ethnicity, Identity and Interaction* (New Delhi: Vikas Publishing House, 1977), pp. 1-7.

[12] Louis Rousselet, *India and its Native Princes: Travels in Central India and in the Presidencies of Bombay and Bengal* (London: Chapman and Hall, 1876), p. 387.

[13] For a brief overview of the different theories regarding the Gonds' place of origins, see Suresh Mishra, *Tribal Ascendancy in Central India: The Gond Kingdom of Garha* (New Delhi: Manak Publications Pvt. Ltd., 2007), pp. 10-11.

[14] Christoph von Fürer-Heimendorf, "The Gond Tribes of India", in *The Gonds of Central India*, ed. Shelagh Weir (London: The British Museum, 1973), p.7.

[15] Detailed accounts of medieval Gond kingdoms—and their interactions with Mughal, Maratha and other outside forces—can be found in the Hindi and English books by the Bhopal-based Indian historian Dr. Suresh Mishra, to whom the author is much indebted for historical guidance.

[16] Stephen Fuchs, *The Gond and Bhumia of Eastern Mandla* (Calcuttta: New Literature Publishing Company, 1960), pp. 14-15; and V.W. Karambelkar, "Literary Activity Under the Gond Rule in Garha-Mandla", *Journal of the Asiatic Society* 19 (1953): pp. 137-44. Although Fuchs identified the Brahmins who served as priests and poets in the Graha-Mandla Gond courts as originating in Benaras, according to Dr. Suresh Mishra—the present-day expert on medieval Gond history—they actually came from Mithila (personal communication).

[17] Muslim Persian terms used by Gond rulers to administer their kingdoms include *diwan* (a high ranking administrative minister), *fauzdar* (a garrison commander), and territorial divisions and subdivisions such as *souba*, *sarkar* and *pargana*.

[18] Hivale, *The Pardhans*, pp. 11-12.

[19] Verrier Elwin (1902-1964) had a long and colourful career in India that defies easy "pigeon-holing". As a young Oxford graduate, he initially came to India as a Church of England missionary, then got involved with Gandhi and the struggle for independence, and thereafter became a scholar of tribal cultures (about which he wrote many seminal books). He married (consecutively) two Gond women with whom he

fathered children, lived most of his life with the Gonds and other tribal communities, became an Indian citizen and in his later years served under Nehru as an official "Advisor on Tribal Affairs". Verrier Elwin's autobiographical texts include *Leaves from the Jungle: A Diary of Life in a Gond Village* (London: John Murray, 1936) and *The Tribal World of Verrier Elwin: An Autobiography* (Bombay and New York: Oxford University Press, 1964). The most extensive biography on Elwin is Ramchandra Guha's *Savaging the Civilized: Verrier Elwin, His Tribals, and India* (New Delhi: Oxford University Press, 1999). Comparatively little has been published to date regarding the less "high profile" career of Elwin's assistant, Shamrao Hivale (1903-1984), whose publications include *The Pardhans of the Upper Narbada Valley*, cited above; *Scholar Gypsy: A Study of Verrier Elwin* (Bombay: M.N. Tripathi, 1946); and (co-authored with Elwin) *Folk Songs of the Maikal Hills* (London: Published for Man in India by H. Milford, Oxford University Press, 1944). Before working with Elwin, Hivale graduated from Wilson College, Bombay, worked as a language teacher to foreign missionaries, and was a friend and activist-follower of Mahatma Gandhi. An informative bio-sketch of Hivale, written by his American son-in-law Thomas R. Carter, can be found at the photographer Sunil Janah's website (http://members.aol.com/sjanah/index-fs.htm).

[20] Umesh Chandra Misra, *Tribal Paintings and Sculptures* (Delhi: B.R. Publishing Corporation, 1989), p.61.

[21] Jangarh and his family were closely connected to Verrier Elwin, both in terms of employment (Adhara Bai's husband—Jangarh's father—was Bhajan Singh Shyam, the Elwin household's cook), and through marriage (Elwin's second wife, Lila, was a cousin of Jangarh's). For further information regarding Dukhala Bai's work for Elwin at Patangarh and its influence on Adhara Bai Shyam, see John H. Bowles et al., "Contemporary Pardhan Gond Art: Iconographic Explanations", *Temenos Academy Review* 10 (London: 2007): p. 92, fn. 2 and 3.

[22] Mathura now falls along the western edge of the modern state of Uttar Pradesh. For further information regarding the ancient origins and evolution of the Krishna myths and cults see Ramkrishna Gopal Bhandarkar, *Vaisnavism, Saivism and Minor Religious Systems* (Strassburg: Karl J. Trübner, 1913) and Romila Thapar, "The Early History of Mathura: Up to and Including the Mauryan Period" in *Mathura,* ed. D.M. Srinivasan (New Delhi, 1989), pp. 12-18.

[23] The "Puranas" (the anglicized plural form of the Sanskrit word *purana*, meaning "of ancient times") are a corpus of important ancient Indian religious and mythological texts—transcribed from yet earlier oral histories—narrating traditional accounts of cosmology, sacred geography, the genealogies and feats of various heroes, kings, saints, divinities, etc.

[24] This quote and illustration (and its sub-caption) from Elwin's *The Tribal Art of Middle India* (London and Bombay: Oxford University Press, 1951), pp. 185-186, and fig. 208; although published in 1951, the book was originally written at Patangarh in 1946.

[25] Serious appreciation of visual expression practiced within India's tribal cultures did not occur before Elwin's mid-century publication of *The Tribal Art of Middle India*. Even Hivale's 1946 roughly coeval publication *The Pardhans of the Upper Narbada Valley*—which likewise illustrates many examples of jewelry and clay reliefs—does not once mention the term "art". Even after India's independence, certain pro-development Indian officials have severely criticized exhibiting tribal forms of visual expression, disdaining them as "backward and ugly objects" (Niloufer Ichaporia, "Crazy for Foreign: The Exchange of Goods and Values on the International Ethnic Arts Market" [UC Berkeley PhD dissertation, 1979], p. 255).

[26] From the author's November 2006 interview with Nankusia Singh Shyam at her home in Professors Colony, Bhopal; translation courtesy of Hartosh Singh Bal.

[27] More specifically, it was Swaminathan's "talent scout" assistant—the photographer Vivek Tembey, then a recent graduate of Gwalior's Fine Arts College—who was the first non-tribal to recognize Jangarh's artistry (in form of a mural he had painted at Patangarh, which depicted the Hindu monkey god Hanuman); and it was Vivek who first encouraged Jangarh to experiment with modern media.

[28] This account of Jangarh and Swaminathan's first meeting in Patangarh was provided by the former head of Bharat Bhavan's Painting Department, the artist Akhilesh Varma, who heard it directly from the astonished driver of the jeep. Also, Jangarh's family were notified of his plans to join Swaminathan in Bhopal at the time of their departure.

[29] The 1988 exhibition at Saitama's Museum of Modern Art was part of Japan's nationwide "Festival of India". Jangarh's residencies at the Mithila Museum were in 1999 and 2001.

[30] The best public collection of Jangarh's early works can be found at Bhopal's Bharat Bhavan, selected works of which are illustrated in Jagdish Swaminathan, *The Perceiving Fingers* (Bhopal: Bharat Bhavan, 1987), figs. 6-31, 40 and 61.

[31] See Gulammohammed Sheikh, "The World of Jangarh Singh Shyam", in *Other Masters: Five Contemporary Folk and Tribal Artists of India*, ed. Jyotindra Jain (New Delhi: Crafts Museum, 1998), p. 17.

[32] Ibid., p. 25.

[33] See Akhilesh's "Pardhan ki 'Mauten'" (in Hindi), Bahuvachan 9, year 3, no. 1 (2001): pp. 104-112; Akhilesh—as an artist, author and individual—prefers to identify himself by his first name only.

[34] From the author's March 2008 interview in Bhopal.

[35] My personal communications on this subject include discussions in New Delhi with the anthropologist and then director of The Crafts Museum, Dr. Jyotindra Jain (who organized a petition to the government to investigate the circumstances of Jangarh's death); the artist and scholar Dr. Niranjan Acharya (Janghar's friend, with whom he regularly stayed during visits to Delhi); and Mustaq Khan (present Deputy Director of The Crafts Museum, New Delhi).

[36] Identified by Nankusia Shyam as Ms. V. Nigam; also identified as Yuko Nigam (see: Prerna Singh Bindra and Deepak Tiwari's "Tragic ending", *The Week*, 22-07-2001, Record Number: A0351923; article available at the website: http://www.cscsarchive.org:8081/MediaArchive/advertise.nsf/%28docid%29/7A447A53E2F83ED1E5256B840036AF2E).

[37] From an unpublished 2006 interview of Nankusia Shyam; translation courtesy of Hartosh Singh Bal.

[38] To date, the most complete published account of the Indian criticisms of the Mithila Museum's treatment of Jangarh is Kavita Singh, "Jangarh Singh Shyam," pp. 62-63. Ultimately, it was the Madhya Pradesh state government which underwrote the cost of transporting Jangarh's body from Japan to Bhopal (Hartosh Singh Bal, "Storytellers of the Night", *Asia Literary Review* 10 [Winter 2008]: p. 40).

[39] Curator Miyoko Hasunuma's 2002 account, entitled "The view at present on the reason why late Mr. Jagadh [sic] Singh Shyam committed suicide" was temporarily posted on the website: http://www.bekkoame.ne.jp/~mithila/010723.html . Deepak Tiwari's short interview of Ms. Hasunuma—entitled "He selected the path of death"—is still available at: http://www.cscsarchive.org:8081/MediaArchive/advertise.nsf/%28docid%29/7A447A53E2F83ED1E5256B840036AF2E . It also bears noting that many of the Mithila Museum's artists-in-residence have felt decently treated during their stints there. The museum's policy is to host at least two Indian artists at a time, and also to provide Indian cooking. Like Jangarh, other artists felt sufficiently positive about their first residency there that they were willing to return for subsequent visits: e.g., at least nine different Mithila painters made repeated visits, some (such as Godaveri Dutta and Baua Devi) returning as many as seven or eight times. (Personal communication, David Szanton, Director of The Ethnic Arts Foundation [see www.mithilapainting.com]).

[40] This list of medications includes Alpex 0.5, Alpix 0.25 and Trika 0.25, which are all versions of an anti-anxiety medication (known elsewhere as "Xanax") frequently and rather casually prescribed in Bhopal to this day.

[41] Akhilesh, "Pardhan ki 'Mauten'", p. 110; translation by Ishwar Dass.

[42] From the author's March 2008 interviews with Akhilesh and Archana Varma.

[43] See Sally Price, *Primitive Art in Civilized Places* (Chicago and London: The University of Chicago Press, 1989).

[44] See Kavita Singh, "Jangarh Singh Shyam," pp. 63-64.

[45] An extensive family tree showing the interrelationship of most of the artists mentioned in this essay can be found in Udayan Vajpeyi and Vivek (Tembey), Jangadh Kalam (Bhopal: Vanya Prakashan, 2006), pp. 208-9.

[46] See for example: B.N. Goswamy's "Pahari Painting: The Family as the Basis of Style", *Marg*, 21 no. 4 (1968): pp. 17-62; Shridhar Andhare's "Mewar Painters, Their Status and Genealogies", in *Facets of Indian Art*, eds. Robert Skelton, Andrew Topsfield, Susan Strong and Rosemary Crill (London: Victoria and Albert Museum, 1986), pp. 176-184; and Tryna Lyons's *The Artists of Nathadwara: The Practice of Painting in Rajasthan* (Bloomington and Ahmedabad: Indiana University Press in association with Mapin Publishing Pvt. Ltd., 2004).

[47] For example, two Bhopal-based artists who are Gond but not Pardhan Gond are the late Sumer Kushram (one of Jangarh's first disciples) and the now Bhopal-based Prasad Singh Kushram (who was also instructed and encouraged by Jangarh).

[48] For a list of forty-nine Bhopal-based Gond artists, see: http://ignca.nic.in/tribal_art_artist_gond.htm.

[49] Notable continuing state patronage of contemporary Gond art and culture is easily apparent in the activities and displays featured at Bhopal's Bharat Bhavan and Indira Gandhi National Museum of Mankind, as well as in the publications and activities of the Bhopal-based Vanya and Madhya Pradesh's Tribal Welfare Department.

[50] Social and political aspects of contemporary Gond art will be more fully addressed in future publications by Rashmi Varma *(Modern Tribal: Indigeneity in Postcolonial India)* and Hartosh Singh Bal (*Waters Close Over Us* [Delhi: HarperCollins, India]). For more regarding the now-burgeoning pan-Gond ethnic/cultural/religious/social/political identity movement (as manifest since 1985 at the Kachhargarh Mela [Kachhargarh Fair]—now the largest annual gathering of Gonds—held at the sacred site of Kachhargarh, Salekasa Tensil, Dist. Bhandara, Maharashtra) see: http://www.indiatogether.org/2006/feb/soc-gonds.htm. For a contemporary Gondwana perspective see Archarya Motiram Kangali, *Gondwana ka Sanskritik Itihaas* (Nagpur, Tirumaii Chandralekha Kangali, 1984) and *Pari Kupaar Lingo Gondi Punem Darshan* (Nagpur: Chandralekha Kangali, 1989).

[51] D.P. Singhal, *India and World Civilization* (London: Pan Macmillan Ltd., 1972), p. xiv.

[52] E.g., see James Clifford, Shelly Errington, Jyotindra Jain and Nelson H. H. Graburn in this book's Suggested Reading section. Such art categories will also be discussed in Wellesley College's April 10, 2010 symposium: "The Gond & Beyond: The Predicament of Contemporary 'Ethnic' Arts".

[53] Like many Gonds, Ram Singh Urveti is not sure about his date of birth. In order to register him at a local school, his brother-in-law claimed that he was born in 1970, but in December 2006 he himself estimated his age to be about forty-one or forty-two years old. Biographical information from a December 2006 interview translated by Ishwar Dass.

[54] The Gorakhpur mentioned here and elsewhere in this book is a town in eastern Madhya Pradesh, not the better-known city in Uttar Pradesh.

[55] From the author's 2005 interview of the artist conducted and translated by Shampa Shah.

[56] From the author's 2006 interview of the artist translated by Ishwar Dass. The claim of endorsement by Jangarh is one of the means that Gond artists now use to promote their status, and usually there is no one around to confirm or deny such claims. As one of Jangahr's closest friends, colleagues and collaborators, Ram Singh Urveti's account of Jangarh's remark has a greater ring of truth than that of other, more junior artists.

[57] On the occasions of Nag Panchmi (a festival honouring snakes), only those of the Urveti *gotra* (clan) get possessed by the Nag Devita (snake god).

[58] These murals were later destroyed when the room in which they were painted was converted into the Museum of Mankind's conservation department. Ram and other Gond artists have painted subsequent murals assigned to them by museum administrators, but these too have been either whitewashed or painted to mask surfaces ruined by (and still subject to) mildew and/or fading. The positive aspect of the museum's continuous if casual approach to commissioning murals by contemporary tribal artists is that it provides the artists with ongoing work and income. But the deterioration or disappearance of certain murals is nonetheless a sad loss to those who appreciate the individual styles of particular Gond artists. Different government agencies find various reasons for commissioning murals by tribal artists; for example, the Municipal Corporation of Bhopal has commissioned Gond and other tribal artists (as well as local school children) to paint murals on walls along public roads (especially upon the high curbs surrounding roundabouts)—as a deterrent to graffiti. Bhajju Shyam and certain other leading contemporary Gond artists have expressed disapproval of such commissions.

[59] A detail of this mural is reproduced in John H. Bowles, "Hybrid Flowerings: A Brief Introduction to Contemporary Pardhan Gond Art", *Temenos Academy Review* 10 (2007): Plate 6.

[60] *The Night Life of Trees* (London: Tara Publishing Ltd., 2003) received the 2008 Bologna Ragazzi Award for New Horizons, a prestigious international children's book award.

[61] Viz.: *Bauhinia vahilii*.

[62] From an interview with the author in December 2006, translated by Ishwar Dass.

[63] Suresh stuffs coloured chalk powder into a cotton cloth, which he then rubs across paper surfaces (often more than one colour will be applied to a single paper)—and thereafter draws in ink. (see Fig. 36)

[64] This painting previously appeared in Udayan Vajpayi and Vivek's *Jangadh Kalam*, p.197.

[65] Suresh's *seedhi* pattern predominantly occurs in his earlier works, and can be seen in the neck area of his Thakur Dev depiction (see colour illustration on p. 31). Suresh and other Gond artists are not alone among "traditional" Indian artists in their ability to vary their styles radically according to different patronage, commissions and markets. For example, the painters of traditional Rajasthani *phads* (large horizontal scrolls illustrating heroic epics) are also capable of working in a number of different styles, including miniature paintings styles, "calendar art" styles, folk art styles and even modernist styles. See Kavita Singh, "Fixed Image in a Changing World: the Phad Paintings of Rajasthan" in *Kingdom of the Sun, Indian Court and Village Art from the Princely State of Mewar*, ed. Joanna Williams (San Francisco: Asian Art Museum, 2007), p. 83.

[66] All quotes of the artist on this page from the author's January 2007 interview, translated by Ishwar Dass.

[67] The natural pigments Durga Bai and other Pardhan Gonds traditionally use for painting their *dignas* and murals include a *hariya rang* (dark green) from the leaves of the semi bean plant, and different-coloured local clays called *rang matti* (for red pigment), *bharri matti* (brown pigment), *ram raj matti* (yellow pigment), *kala matti* (black and dark gray pigments) and *chhuhi matti* (white pigments).

[68] *Janam Ashtami* refers to the "eight days around the birth" celebrating Krishna's birth, and relates to the Atekanhaiyya (a.k.a. Kanhaiya Athen) festival. (See p. 20 of this essay). According to the artist Rajendra Singh Shyam, the traditional murals celebrating Krishna's birth—depicting Krishna in the centre of a herd of cows, or dancing with the *gopis* (maiden cowherders) on Kanhaiy Athe (the eighth day of the waning moon in the month of Bhado [July-August])—are now being replaced by the simple posting of "photographs" (calendar art depictions) on the walls.

[69] See Bowles et al., "Contemporary Pardhan Gond Art", p. 97. According to Mustaq Khan, *nag mori* is also used as a generic term for any pattern or design based on serpent tracks (personal communication).

[70] Durga Bai's illustrations appear in the following books: Sirish Rao and Anushka Ravishankar, *One, Two, Tree!* (London: Tara Publishing Ltd.,

2003); *The Night Life of Trees*; Begum Rokheya Sakhawat Hossain, *Sultana's Dream* (London: Tara Publishing Ltd., 2005); and Vijay Chaurasia, *Aakhyaan: Gond Janjati ke Katha Itihas ka Sakshya*, ed. Ashok Mishra and Kapil Tiwari (Bhopal: Adivasi Lok Kala Academy, 2006)—which also features illustrations by Ram Singh Urveti and Narmada Prasad.

71 See Chaitanya Sambrani, *Edge of Desire: Recent Art in India* (London: Philip Wilson Publishers, 2005), cat. no. 28, pp. 120-121. It should be noted that, although the text accompanying the illustration of this artwork mentions that Subhash's painting has "overtones" relating to 9/11, the depicted theme was actually inspired by a local event occurring decades earlier. See John H. Bowles's "Visual Dialogue Between the East and West", *Biblio* 11, nos. 11-12 (November – December 2006): p. 32.

72 This sculpture previously appeared in Udayan Vajpeyi and Vivek's *Jangadh Kalam* (Bhopal: Tribal Welfare Department, Madhya Pradesh, 2006), p. 189.

73 Rajendra's siblings include a sister and two deceased brothers .

74 Although both Rajendra and Sushila are Pardhan Gonds, their respective clans (his the Shyam clan, hers the Marabi) are forbidden to intermarry; see Hivale, *The Pardhans*, pp. 30-31.

75 Viz., *Shorea robusta*.

76 From the author's November 2006 interview, translated by Hartosh Singh Bal.

77 Over the past two decades, Rajendra Shyam has participated in various exhibitions and workshops organized in New Delhi by TRIFED (the Ministry of Tribal Affairs, Government of India) and The Crafts Museum, and in Bhopal by Adivasi Lok Kala Sangrahalaya and Bharat Bhavan. As this book goes to press (November, 2009), he is making his first trip abroad to attend an exhibition of his and Venkat Raman Singh Shyam's paintings at the New Art Exchange, Nottingham, UK.

78 Although Sushila Shyam often extensively collaborates with her husband in the execution of artworks, she prefers that her contributions remain anonymous and thus does not co-sign their work. See John H. Bowles's "Tradition and Modernity—A Two Way Street", in *The Magic Makers* (New Delhi: The Academy of Fine Arts and Literature, 2009), p. 268.

79 Many of the artists (and other Gonds) vividly speak of the long—and ever-increasing—treks necessary for gathering fuel-wood from the nearest jungle. While their different estimates of distances may vary considerably, there is no question that the jungle has been dramatically receding over the past half-century, due to extensive local timbering for fuel-wood and other household needs.

80 From a November 2006 interview translated by Ishwar Dass.

81 See Crispin Bates's Race, *Caste and Tribe in Central India: The Early Origins of Indian Anthropolmetry, Edinburgh papers in South Asian Studies* no. 3 (Edinburgh: University of Edinburgh, 1995), p.18.

82 *The London Jungle Book* was illustrated by Bhajju Shyam and co-authored with Sirish Rao and Gita Wolf (London: Tara Publishing in Association with The Museum of London, 2004).

83 See the Gond artist Venkat Raman Singh Shyam, *The Flying Elephant* (Fig. 17) for his account of this myth Also see Verrier Elwin, *Myths of Tribal India* (Bombay: Oxford University Press, 1949), pp. 203-204 and 218; and V. Bhattacharyya and G.K. Shrigondekar, "Sanskrit Works on Elephants", *Journal of the Bihar and Orissa Research Society* 10, 317.ff.

84 *The London Jungle Book* was preceded by other Gond-illustrated books by Tara Publications, including Anushka Ravishankar and Sirish Rao's *One, Two, Tree!* (2003), illustrated by Durga Bai; and Kanchana Arni and Gita Wolf's *Beasts of India* (2003), which included illustrations by Bhajju Shyam, Durga Bai, Prasad Khusharam and Jangarh and Nandkusiya [sic] Singh Shyam. Subsequent publications include: Gita Wolf-Sampath and Sirish Rao, *The Night Life of Trees* (2006), featuring illustrations by Bhajju Shyam, Ram Singh Urveti and Durga Bai; Begum Rokheya Sakhawat Hossain's *Sultana's Dream* (2005), illustrated by Durga Bai; and Sirish Rao's *That's How I See Things* (2007) and *Flight of the Mermaid* (2009), illustrated by Bhajju Shyam.

85 E.g., Bhajju's works have been exhibited at Musée des Arts Decoratifs (Paris, 1998), The Museum of London (London, 2004), Horniman Museum (London, 2005), Paris Book Fair (Paris, 2006), The Rebecca Hossack Art Gallery (London, 2006) and the Turin Book Fair (Turin, 2007). Bhajju Shyam has also executed major commissions, such as a series of large ceiling panels he painted in December 2004 through January 2005 to hang above the main entrance/lobby of New Delhi's five-star Ashok Hotel. His more recent projects include embellishing furniture designed by a south Delhi-based company named Kaaru.

86 Of all the biographical interviews of artists done in preparation for this essay, Venkat's was by far the longest and most detailed: its transcription totaled almost 17,000 words and entailed three separate interview sessions. Only a small portion of that information appears in this essay.

87 Venkat's uncle Jawahar was a school teacher who died at the age of twenty-six; among his personal effects was a sketch book filled with realistic/modern-style drawings of film stars.

[88] The artworks that Venkat executed (between 2001-2003) can be seen at Madhya Pradesh's tourist hotels in Pachmari, Riva, Jabalpur, Satna, Chitrakut, Khajuraho, Chhindwara, the Pench National Park, Gwalior, Chanderi, Indore, Ujjain, Jhabua and Bhedaghat.

[89] To date, Venkat has shown his work several times abroad: once in Spain (at Forum Barcelona 2004), and thrice in the UK (at Oxford in 2006 [through Art in Action, a London-based NGO]; in 2007 in London and Scotland [through a tour organized by the Adivasi Arts Trust and West Highland Animation]; and at Nottingham's New Art Exchange in 2009 [organized by the Adivasi Arts Trust]). In April 2010 he makes his first trip to the USA to participate in this exhibition's opening and its related symposium, and his first foreign solo exhibition—entitled "The Tribal World of Venkat Raman Singh Shyam"—at the Brookline Arts Center (a nonprofit institution near Boston).

[90] Venkat had just arrived in the neighborhood to attend an art auction at the Taj Hotel, organized by the OSIAN's Group (including three of his paintings and works by many other artists). Although this was his first experience of terrorism, it was not his first exposure to five-star hotels; in 2005-2006 he executed two hundred painted silk hangings for the Taj Hotel Group's affiliated Chandela Taj Hotel, at Khajuraho.

[91] "Vanya", a Bhopal-based institution established in March 1980 by the Madhya Pradesh state government for the promotion of tribal art and culture, has recently instituted an annual Rs 25,000 "Madhya Pradesh Jangarh Puraskar" award and citation. The first recipient was the Patangarh-born Dilip Shyam, who received this award on February 1, 2008, as part of the celebration of a three-day International Tribal Film Festival in Indore, Madhya Pradesh. The state's Tribal Welfare Minister Kunwar Vijay Shah also serves as Vanya's Chairman. Additional prize-giving institutions range from official branches of the Madhya Pradesh state government—now under the control of the Bharatiya Janata Party (BJP)—to the New Delhi-based Lalit Kala Akademi (National Fine Arts Academy), which has its own longtime ideological and political affiliations with India's national Congress party. The various means of government control or political influence regarding cultural perceptions in general—and recognition and state patronage of the arts of significant minority groups in particular—is a complex topic now being pursued by Rashmi Varma at the University of Warwick.

[92] Since the early 1970s, the category of "Outsider Art" has been loosely applied by art critics and dealers (e.g., Hervé Perdriolle's aforementioned Outsider Art Gallery in Pondicherry) to various forms of contemporary tribal art; but the term more properly applies to isolated or marginalized self-taught artists who produce eccentric work that does not conform to the established traditions of any particular community, or to more mainstream modern/postmodern art movements.

[93] Over recent years examples of Mayank's work have been included in some major contemporary exhibitions, such as *Freedom: Sixty Years After Indian Independence*, organized by the Kolkata-based Centre of International Modern Art. See illustration and accompanying text in the exhibition catalogue of that same title (Kolkata: Art and Heritage Foundation, 2007), pp.66-67 and Sotheby's July 17, 2007 *Indian Art: An Auction to Benefit the Kolkata Museum of Modern Art* (New York: Sotheby: July 17, 2007), pp. 66-67.

[94] From the author's January 2007 interview, translated by Ishwar Dass.

[95] Hivale, *The Pardhans*, p. 222.

[96] This painting and its accompanying texts were previously reproduced in *Temenos Academy Review* 10 (London: 2007), Plate 3 and pp. 94-95; and in the *Asian Literary Review* no. 10 (Winter 2008): p. 36.

[97] This painting has been previously reproduced in *Asian Literary Review* 10 (Winter 2008): p. 37.

[98] Jangarh inscribed this image: "हरणवा का पेड़", a slight phonetic misspelling of "हरडवा का पेड़" (*haradva* tree), which is also called *harada* in colloquial Gond dialect, *harra* in Hindi, and is botanically identified as *Chebullic myrobanan*, and/or *Terminalia chebula*; (identification courtesy of Venkat Raman Singh Shyam).

[99] This print was originally acquired at Bharat Bhavan in the late 1980s by Stuart Cary Welch (the renowned curator, scholar and collector of Indian art), and thereafter gifted to the author.

[100] The earliest written transcript of this Gond creation myth appears in R.V. Russell and Rai Bahadur Hira Lal's *The Tribes and Castes of the Central Provinces of India*, Vol. III (London: Macmillan, 1916), pp. 49-50.

[101] Although the Gonds' Creation of the Earth myth typically casts Bara Deo (Shiva) as the creator, Jangarh clearly inscribed this painting "Brahma-ji"—here casting the god Brahma in the role of creator, in accord with Puranic creation mythology.

[102] This reproduction includes painted margins which Jangarh himself had folded back to secure onto a canvas stretcher, and then disregarded in the course of completing his work on this canvas (thus the unfinished details and blemishes along the painting's margins and tacking edges). Measurements featured in catalogue entry do not include tacking edges.

[103] Regarding medieval Gond dynasties and kingdoms, see the writings of the historian Suresh Mishra (e.g., *Tribal Ascendancy in Central India: The Gond Kingdom of Garha* [New Delhi: Manak Pub., 2007]). Mythological accounts of Raja Heera Khan Chhatri can be found in Verrier Elwin, *Folk Tales of the Mahakoshal* (London: Oxford University Press, 1944), pp. 82-87, and Vijay Chourasia, *Khyaan: Gond Janjaati ke Katha Itihaas ka Sakshya* (Bhopal: Adivasi Lok Kala Akademi, 2006), pp. 429-509.

[104] *Ficus glomerata*; see Hivale, *The Pardhans*, p. 224.

[105] The *baans* or bamboo here referred to is *Dendrocalamus strictus*; the *saja* or "crocodile-bark" tree is *Terminalia alata*.

[106] This photograph appears in Elwin, *The Tribal Art of Middle India*, fig. 78, p. 75. Its accompanying caption (on p. 74) reads: "Gond marriage-post from Mandla, with red and blue dots on a white ground, glass teeth and cowrie eyes. The wood is *Shorea rubusta* and the post stands 60 inches above the ground."

[107] This entry's information regarding Karma songs has been drawn from Verrier Elwin's *Folk Songs of the Maikal Hills* (London: Oxford University Press, 1944), pp. 3-26.

[108] *Ficus religiosa*.

[109] This painting was gifted by the author to Dr. Arthur F. Jones and Dr. Crystal Hui-Shu Yang, professors in the Department of Art and Design, University of North Dakota, Grand Forks, ND.

[110] Kumbha Mela literally means "pot fair", and is the world's largest religious gathering, held on an annual rotating basis at four sacred north Indian cities. The "pot" referred to is that from which *amrit* (elixir of immortality) was spilled following the *samudra manthan* (mythic churning of the ocean).

[111] This painting previously appeared (in an unfinished state) in Vajpayi and Vivek, *Jangadh Kalam*, p. 167.

[112] This painting and its accompanying explanation were originally published in *Temenos Academy Review* 10, plate 8; pp. 100-101.

[113] The "silk-cotton tree", *Bombax cieba / Bombax malabaricum*.

[114] *Madhuca latifolia*.

[115] Venkat was personally well acquainted with Jadish Swaminathan, the late Indian Primitivist artist and first director of Bhopal's Bharat Bhavan. Swaminathan often used the silhouette of a lone crow as a recurrent "signature" image in his paintings and sculpture. This tribute by a Gond tribal artist to a modern Primitivist thus provides a most unusual example of cultural influences coming "full circle".

[116] *Anthus similis*.

[117] The "Indian laurel tree", *terminalia tomentosa*.

[118] See Salim Ali's *The Book of Indian Birds* Vol. 2 (Bombay: Bombay Natural History Society and Oxford University Press, 1941), p. 43. The *tithi* or redwattled lapwing is scientifically identified as *Vanellus indicus*.

[119] This *chaar* or *achaar* tree has been identified as *Buchanania lanzan*—a member of the mango family. It has "...an almond-like stone containing a nut known as *chironji* in the trade. Traditionally used as an essential ingredient in a good *kheer* (rice-pudding), and because *chironji* nuts sell so dearly, a vital source of earning for tribals in central India." (Pradip Krishen, personal communication).

[120] The "silk-cotton tree", *Bombax cieba / Bombax malabaricum*.

[121] The *salhe* tree (a.k.a. *salai*) can be identified as *Boswellia serrata*. It is known as the "Indian frankincense tree" on account of its fragrant gum. (Identification courtesy of Pradip Krishen.)

[122] This painting previously appeared in Udayan Vajpayi and Vivek's *Jangadh Kalam*, p.157.

[123] The "silk-cotton tree", *Bombax cieba / Bombax malabaricum*.

[124] In rural India, clothes are customarily washed by being soaked and then beaten upon a rock.

[125] Aheers are a caste of herdsmen and milkmen.

[126] See explanation on p. 30

[127] *Kodon* and *kutki* are two millets (*Paspalum scrobiculatum* and *Panicum psilipodium* or *milaceum*, respectively); see Hivale, *The Pardhans*, p. 224-225.

[128] This is the same Bhim who appears in the Mahabarata epic.

[129] Viz.: Bhopal's Indira Gandhi National Museum of Mankind.

[130] *Ficus religiosa*.

[131] *Ficus religiosa*.

[132] "The Best of the Best" is based on a traditional Gond story first recorded by Verrier Elwin at Churi Zamindari and Dist. Mandla. Entitled "The Wagtail and the Mouse", the story appears in Elwin's *Folk Tales of the Mahakoshal* (London: Oxford University Press, 1944), pp. 468-470.

[133] See: www.westhighlandanimation.co.uk.

[134] The story depicted in the film "How the Elephant Lost His Wings" was based on a Saora tribal account of the flying elephant myth, found by Tara Douglas in Verrier Elwin's *Tribal Myths of Orissa* (London: Oxford University Press, 1954), p. 380. The Pardhan Gond artist Venkat Raman Singh Shyam also shared his version of this story with Douglas.

[135] The Ghadwa (also spelt Ghadva and Gadwa) are an artisan community that has long provided ritual metal figurines to certain Gond communities. Their ambiguous ethnicity is of probable tribal origin, and they consider themselves to be *adivasi* (tribal). See Zarine Cooper and Michel Postel, *Bastar Folk Art: Shrines, Figures and Memorials* (Mumbai: Project for Indian Cultural Studies, Publication VIII, 1999), p. 3; and Swaminathan, *The Perceiving Fingers*, pp. 45-46.

[136] See: www.talleststory.com/adivasiartstrust/index.html

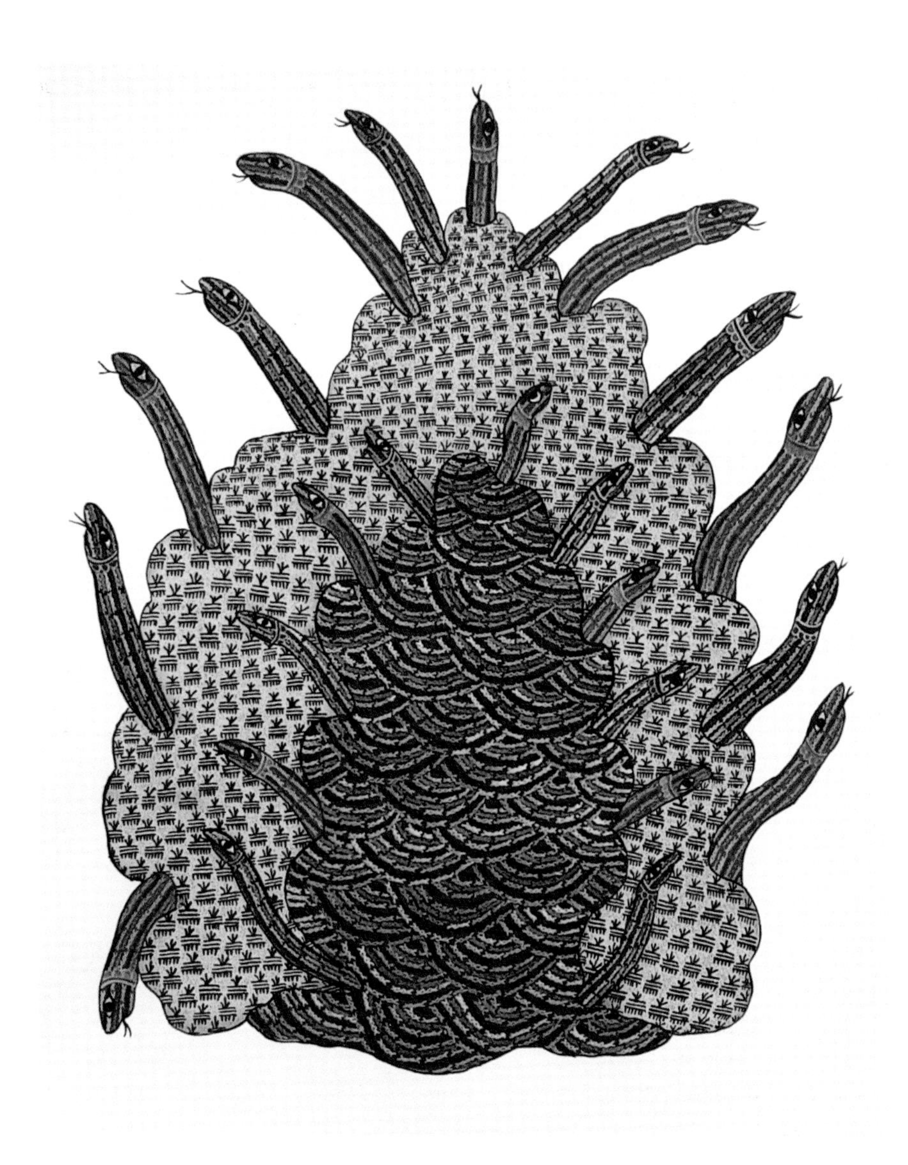

***Putti** (2003) by Rajendra Shyam, Acrylic on paper, 24½ x 19½".*

A putti *(termite hill) is often inhabited by cobras, which are given offerings and worshipped at the Nagpanchmi festival. Here the central smaller mound features the artist's* bandha *("tied") pattern, and the blue mound features a repeated tattoo pattern.*

SUGGESTED READING

Akhilesh. "*Pardhan ki 'Mauten'*" (in Hindi). Bahuvachan 9, year 3, no. 1 (2001): pp. 104-112.

Bowles, John H. "Hybrid Flowerings: A Brief Introduction to Contemporary Pardhan Gond Art". *Temenos Academy Review* 10 (2007): pp. 80-90.

—— et al. "Contemporary Pardhan Gond Art: Iconographic Explanations". *Temenos Academy Review* 10 (2007): pp. 91-102.

Clifford, James. *The Predicament of Culture: Twentieth-Century Ethnography, Literature, and Art.* Cambridge, MA and London: Harvard University Press, 1988.

Elwin, Verrier. *The Tribal Art of Middle India*. London: Oxford University Press, 1951.

Errington, Shelly. *The Death of Authentic Primitive Art and Other Tales of Progress*. Berkeley: University of California Press, 1998.

Graburn, Nelson H.H., ed. *Ethnic and Tourist Arts: Cultural Expressions from the Fourth World*. Berkeley: University of California Press, 1976.

Hivale, Shamrao. *The Pardhans of the Upper Narbada Valley*. London: Oxford University Press, 1946.

Kramrisch, Stella. *Unknown India: Ritual Art in Tribe and Village*, 1968. Exhibition catalogue, Philadelphia Museum of Art.

Martin, Jean-Hubert et al. *Magiciens de la terre*, 1989. Exhibition catalogue, Musée National D'Art Moderne, Centre Georges Pompidou, Paris.

Price, Sally. *Primitive Art in Civilized Places*. Chicago and London: The University of Chicago Press, 1989.

Rossi, Barbara. *From the Ocean of Painting: India's Popular Paintings, 1589 to the Present.* New York and Oxford: Oxford University Press, 1998.

Sheikh, Gulammohammed. "The World of Jangarh Singh Shyam". In *Other Masters: Five Contemporary Folk and Tribal Artists of India*, edited by Jyotindra Jain. New Delhi: Crafts Museum, 1998, pp. 16-33.

Singh, Kavita. "Jangarh Singh Shyam and the Great Machine". *Marg: A Magazine of the Arts* 53, no. 2 (December 2001): pp. 60-64.

Swaminathan, Jagdish. *The Perceiving Fingers*. Bhopal: Bharat Bhavan, 1987.

Vajpeyi, Udayin and Vivek. *Jangadh Kalam*. Bhopal: Vanya Prakashan and Madhya Pradesh Tribal Welfare Department, Hindi edition 2006, English edition 2008.

***Rai ki Dhaniya* (Eagle)**, *2003, by Rajendra Shyam, Acrylic on paper, 21 x 17½".*

INDEX

(Note: As much as possible, the spelling of foreign terms and names—when transcribed from interviews with the Pardhan Gond artists—conforms to either the artists' preferred spellings, or transliterations of their own pronunciations by the translators. For example, Venkat Raman Singh Shyam's "Arawat" has been retained, rather than using any of the more widespread Sanskrit-based spellings, such as "Airawat", "Airawata", "Airavat" or "Airavata".)

PICTURE CREDITS

JOHN H. BOWLES: pp. 3, 9,18, 20, 27, 30, 32, 33 (bottom), 34-35, 38, 42, 47 (bottom), 81 (bottom), 93, 95, 106, 108 & 116.

OLGA BOWLES and BLAKE PRAYTOR, Department of Visual and Performing Arts at Greenville Technical College, Greer, South Carolina: pp. 1, 6, 11, 15, 25, 29, 31 (right), 41 (right), 44, 46, 48 (right), 50, 52, 55, 60-61, & 94.

STEVE BRIGGS, Briggs PhotoGraphics: pp. 71, 83 & 84.

VERRIER ELWIN: photographs on pp. 41 (left) & 56, and drawing on p. 21 (from Verrier Elwin, *The Tribal Art of Middle India*, Figs. 78, 96 & 208; with permission of Oxford University Press).

PRAKASH HATVALNE: p. 16 and back cover.

LESLIE MACKENZIE, West Highland Animation: photograph and cel image on p. 97.

EDGARD RINCON: pp. 2, 6, 12, 19, 31 (left), 33 (top), 36-37, 40, 43, 47 (top), 48 (left), 49, 51, 53-54, 57-59, 63-65, 68-69, 73, 75, 77, 78-79, 80 (top), 85-92 & 96.

PUJA SAXENA: p. 115

VENKAT RAMAN SINGH SHYAM: pp. 66-67.
The photograph on p. 22 was earlier published, without credit, in the illustrated catalogue *J. Swaminathan: Exhibition of Paintings* (New Delhi, Vadehra Art Gallery, 1993); due diligence was shown in tracing the still unknown identity of the photographer—who is welcome to notify the publisher for acknowledgment in future editions.

Inaugural meeting for Tribal Art and Heritage Projects, Bhopal Chapter of the Indian National Trust for Art and Cultural Heritage; March 14, 2009.
From left to right: Dr. Meera Dass, Suresh Singh Dhurvey, Ram Singh Urveti, John H. Bowles, Rajendra Shyam, Bhajju Shyam, Durga Bai Vyam, Subhash Vyam, Dr. Ishwar Dass, Dr. Suresh Mishra, Venkat Raman Singh Shyam, Shambhu Dhyaal Shyam and Mayank Shyam.